INCRE

LIES

INCREDIBLE LIES

A Fond Look Back at Old-Fashioned Golf

THOMAS VAUGHAN

Peregrine Productions

ISBN 0–97269-48–1 paperback
ISBN 978–0–97269-48-0
ISBN 0–97269-48–2–x hardback
ISBN 978–0–97269-48–7
Publisher: Peregrine Productions
Printed in the United States of America

This is a work of fiction.
The events described here are imaginary.
Although parts of the book are based on real experiences of the author,
it should be assumed the settings and characters are fictitious
and do not represent specific places or living or dead persons.
Any resemblance is entirely coincidental.

DEDICATION

MY EVERLASTING THANKS
TO THE
FOLLOWING FOURSOMES

Daniel Kathryn Kathleen & Mary
Richard John Daniel & Gerry
Thomas W. Peter T. Paul B. & Chauncey T.
Garry B. Paul E. Rev. Paul M. & Hon. J.B.
BTH Ted H. Mario S. & John McC

To my coach, caddie and counselor
EAPC-V, LP
&
Meagan Margot Stephen & Cameron
&
Hildegarde

PLAYERS TO THE HILT

CONTENTS

INCREDIBLE LIES

On the golf course, a man may be the dogged victim of inexorable fate,
but struck down by an appalling stroke of tragedy,
become the hero of an unbelievable melodrama,
or the clown in a side-splitting comedy.

ROBERT TYRE JONES

THE PRELUDE

During my professional life I have written about events large and small, almost always on a deadline—plagues, pogroms, stock plunges, insurrections, the rise of champions and the horrendous fall of persons and powers from dizzying heights to rocky places. You name it. Unlike Proust and his tribe, I rarely draw on my own experience; my self seldom comes into play. Not during working hours anyway. That was not authorial, not germane, or professional.

My steady assignment was to speedily form and authenticate no-non-sense stories—*what happened* and *why*, in sharp, bright, declarative sentences. Kansas City style. And boy did I love it! But now I am more than ready for some no-deadline, low-profile years. So why am I already at my old desk, looking out the big clean window of my new library staring down into the flotsam borne on the incoming tide. There's a lot of exotic clutter there in spring, much like my mind these last three days.

This was a clarion wake-up call out of nowhere, with me determined to get it all down on paper before it vanishes, pondering and plumbing my past. This was new to me, my own recollections . . . who would have supposed?

First, let me say that whenever you climb into a big touring car for a country road trip, the unexpected dependably signs on as a silent partner. Particularly so when you have impulsively stashed a full golf bag in the trunk. This marks my departure point for several fond looks backward and all around. Let me explain.

. . . .

There I was, behind the wheel, driving the lazy curves of the downriver highway. The air was still and balmy. It was the edge of spring and I was dreaming Wordsworth's dreams. Far down below the banks, the noble river pursued a stately course generally west, a vast estuary at last rushing headlong into the cold Pacific far out beyond the surf.

Just over the rocky brow of a long curving hill, an imperious flag woman brought me up short of her road crew. Some blackened trees from last summer's fires were being felled on the slope above the road. The traffic controller cut a striking picture as long blond hair tumbled from her day-glo orange helmet. Her dark green shades impassively fixed on me. Her long cigarette holder and jets of smoke rising from finely turned nostrils caused bemusement. The outdoors had not yet been declared a non-smoking area.

As I followed the smoke stream eddying up toward her pennant, I lined up on the flag of her partner far along the highway. But then a country mile off, beyond the road crew, another flag fluttered, a small red slash in the dark green trees. There was no doubt about it. A golf flag on some hidden green.

A tree crashed to earth above me.

INCREDIBLE LIES

"Move on!" the lady emphatically commanded, but my impatience had given way to curiosity. My wife and I had driven back and forth along this road during our fall and winter search for a downriver hideaway. We had given no thought to any games, let alone golf. No notice had ever been given to available golf courses, nor had we ever discussed the game as a necessary part of life in the country. I say this, even while noting that I had, in the very last gasps of our move, thrown my just-acquired clubs and gear into the car for lack of a better idea.

It's all a bit curious in reflection. Anyway, a couple of miles along the road I'd taken, impulse took over. I cranked the wheel hard right, spinning onto a graveled road heading up into the dense forest.

To what? No quaint finger pointed or guidepost beckoned, but I easily found my way through the labyrinth of cedar and fir stands. Like a horse to the barn. Then dramatically (for me, anyway), it was revealed: a piece of undiscovered landscape. I was in golf country—nine undulating holes, hilly in fact. Not a seaside links, but a Scottish scramble!

The scarred parking lot was empty except for some hard-used golf carts and a vintage tractor attached to somewhat rusted mowers. Through the trees down to the south, the river lazed along home, and in the foreground were some tended slopes. Fairways beyond doubt.

So I pulled out my bag and sauntered down toward what might be an elusive first tee, much cut up by a host of obviously enthusiastic players. An eerie sense of anticipation had already infused me, a strange combination of serenity and excitement. Standing there in solitary splendor, I sucked in the salty maritime air. Breathing hard almost brought me to my knees with a hard punch of memory, pricked by the wind-driven odors eddying from years long past. There was the firm grip and then the intense release, the surge of long pent-up energies thought to be gone.

But let's face it; we all know the sudden discovery of a secret golf course elates players of any age; those hidden curves and slopes and swells, the challenges suddenly revealed, the wind and sun and soft turf underfoot. Ecstasy! Wolfe is wrong. You *can* find home again. Sometimes.

Now the weather-beaten clubhouse beckoned; ramshackle cedar shingles and shake roof hugging the slope in rustic perfection. A phlegmatic attendant hunkered down behind the used ball counter was engrossed in some TV tournament replay. He was holed up in his casual shop, laid snug beside an even more casual-looking golf course. Spotting a stranger, however, he instantly detached himself and courteously introduced himself as the owner, greenskeeper, pro—"take your choice." But then he gave me a longer and more appraising sidewise stare. It's a fact; pros have special insight—the ones who last, anyway.

"We have a pretty sporty nine here," he stated, intrigued and somehow approving of my casual dress. Yes, the first muster was passed—the mysteriously right clothes. Actually, throughout my sabbatical I had always dressed as though an unhurried afternoon of golf was my next and best objective, or maybe a whole day or weekend.

My clubs, all seventeen, looked right, as did the heavy canvas no-nonsense bag into which they were choked. (Three over the limit, I was later informed.) Certainly my ancient, much-loved brown leather spikes had seen hard service on many great fairways. And also my ageless bomber jacket was back in style—a long-ago gift from a special friend. Twenty minutes ago I was homeward bound; now there was an inexorable movement toward a game almost forgotten. And all this without a Faustian pact.

Neatly sidestepping the pro's engaging small talk, I described myself as "one of those very private persons, devoted to shots, not handicaps."

"What *is* your handicap then?" he asked.

I replied that I was carrying a big one. "A full generation layoff from the great game." I almost lost myself counting back so far. Some handicap!

The pro grinned and waved me back toward the lonely first tee jutting over the fairway awash with markers and grass fragments.

"Go play nine on the house, son, and then tell me what you think of Firclad."

"What's that?" I asked innocently.

"The name of this course, *my* course. I laid it out," the owner modestly announced, his sunny face a mass of genial furrows, much creased by hard winds and work. A seventy-plus optimist with blue eyes and big, hewed hands. "Merry and bright" seemed my best theme with him.

"Okay. If I have a hole in one I'll report to you and buy the drinks. That is, if you can serve celebratory drinks."

"I've never had one either," he quipped, as he shagged off toward a cedar-battened house snugged down and relaxed in mossy beds of ferns along the wooded hillside, just above the starting tee. A perfect site for his lair.

And why should I explain my hiatus to anyone, really? Almost a forty-year recess. Or how to relate now that a few days ago the chauffeur of a dear old duffer friend had suddenly delivered me this bag choked with clubs, plus a couple dozen balls in plastic wrap to boot? A truly God-awful player, my ancient Magoo friend had that previous afternoon made every person's dream shot on the city's best tournament course. Perfect in that he at last made a hole in one. His drive careened off a hardwood tree, burrowing through the largest trap guarding the greens. His dazed and mutilated ball had then dribbled and staggered across the long green, made an agonizing and most unlikely full turn around and dropped down into the cup.

Yes, an ace! And right in front of a gaping throng of Thursday afternoon low-handicap players, each eager to applaud in return for all the traditional, endless free drinks Alger would stand his bemused fellows.

Mercifully, someone had reminded Alger to play out eight and nine and avoid bad luck. He had then obediently scored a double and triple bogie, more familiar numbers on his card. There was no doubt he would now die happy; meanwhile explaining and recounting to an ever-diminishing circle of benumbed friends how he had "conquered the seventh." And so he had. To be so lucky! And so many had witnessed his "skill!"

The next day my Alger's "old clubs" arrived as a gift on my doorstep. Why, I don't know. Alger had re-outfitted himself: cavernous bag, seventeen clubs, and a powerful electric cart to haul it all—huge, a recreational vehicle designed really for Indianapolis racing. Maybe he had sensed my need to re-engage.

Yes, early in our golfing century the peerless Harry Vardon said it best:

"No matter what happens, never stop hitting the ball." How true, how true.

INCREDIBLE
LIES

THE FIRST HOLE

So there I was, standing stalwart and serene on the first tee at Firclad, a sequestered links in as yet undiscovered country. And I must emphasize *country*. Explaining the layout to me, the ruddy pro reported that his lower four holes were originally a cow pasture long known to be part of an ancient Indian hunting camp for bear, deer, elk, and swans. He had bought the cleared land from a morose Finnish farmer who had lost too many of his prized Holsteins toppling end over udders down the steeply sloped cut-over ravines.

Happily, my golf bag also yielded a worn glove just made for my left hand, and I pulled out Alger's long driver, heavily stained with the white marks of his endless topped and shanked endeavors. Despite all, persimmon wood has special éclat. Alger had groomed his clubs.

Then, with some panache learned at my father's knickered knee, I salvaged a wood tee still embedded in the much-abused turf and casually tossed some scarce blades of dew-laden grass up for a wind check. About force three on the Beaufort scale, I thought. The corner of my peripheral vision picked up a big view window glimmering in the fir trees, the den from which my pro obviously patrolled his fairways. Though deep in his lair, he could surely see me up close with such heavy binoculars. I stretched languidly and took my ease, more or less, as very private persons are wont to do. Already lots of kinks and strains, and more tomorrow for sure.

Would he guess? Could he spot my vintage stance? And was it still called a caddie swing? . . . Were there even any caddies anymore, except in TV tournaments? Could he spot my dated idiosyncrasies of thirty . . . wait a minute . . . it was actually thirty-five years, three months and four days to the very afternoon! Yes, it had to be. After all, this was suddenly mid-May in the mid-nineties. I gazed aloft, still engrossed in correcting my simple subtraction of mounting decades.

Just then in my peripheral vision at about one o'clock an immense white-headed eagle sprang from a snag, up near what appeared to be maybe the fifth or sixth hillside fairway far above me. At least a seven-foot wingspread. Surely a Roman omen from the past! Here on this Tarpeian rock it would appear that the gods remembered great games of long ago and once again might be well disposed. To me, soaring eagles could well mean good omens—an afternoon of Roman glory. Feverish golfers snatch at such signs like high priests. It had almost been so the last time.

"Last time" was forty-six plus years ago and almost three thousand miles away, near the Atlantic shoreline rather than the curling surf of the North Pacific coast. And it had been a renowned course to remember forever . . . even then a true test of endurance in golf. Maybe too much so. But it was all so clear to me, this moment. . . .

. . . .

Just a week preceding that far-off game of memory, some Philadelphia friends had cleverly introduced me to their famous Merion course, and on a weekend to boot. The Ardmore crowd and others on Philadelphia's

Main Line had a swank, rather say ponderous attitude toward golf in general. This almost stifled my urge to play the legendary course. But I pulled myself together and racked up two dramatic birdies on the ninth and eighteenth holes. The ninth is a wicked par three, with an elusive green guarded by vast pits of sand. But with a burst of great luck and verve, my nine iron shot hit in the folds of the flag and sank down beside the cup. Oh my! So close to perfection, even as Merion is close to heaven.

At dinner that evening, our dates had giggled and looked disbelieving when halfway through the filets I stated that I carried my hickory-shafted nine wherever I intended to play. My host was oddly shocked, needlessly so. But then regions and wit differ, or so I thought back then. And of course, so do golf courses, for certain. I never played Merion again.

Then on the following Thursday, back in New Haven, I took my last final exam at Yale; a grand romp in my favorite—Roman history. The one big question posed was made to order for me: the First Punic War and the details of Hannibal's encounter battle at Lake Trasimene. Soon after this lucky triumph, my special golf and gin pal honked outside my rooms in his battered convertible.

We were bound through the New Haven elms for "a round" at the magnificent, but little-known Yale Golf Course, an extravagantly wonderful spread of eighteen grueling holes. Wordsworth was right, "bliss was it . . . to be alive." We pranced on to the back nine first, like Scottish deer. One must see it to fully understand our somewhat exalted state. Like the Sahara, Siberia, and the South Atlantic, the magnificent fairways encased in lush new foliage were vast, beautiful, and empty. We wanted for nothing. Time and space were ours. An afternoon to savor, to remember, as I did with ease even now, far to the west.

THE FIRST HOLE

3

We loved our golfing days. They were to me "the dear old days at Yale." For three school years my friend and I had mused and nurtured each other while carrying a secret post-war pride, more specifically a fantasy, that but for that pitiless, inhuman war some odd savants outrageously called "the recent unpleasantness," we might have become gentlemen golf pros trailing Sam Snead and his pals across endless emerald greens.

My stoic golf partner's dream was rudely shattered over Vienna in 1944 when a medal-mad colonel wheeled the few survivors in his flock of B-25s on yet a third calamitous pass up the Danube and across the shattered Vienna Woods, on to the imperial town. Seconds later a gutsy ME 109 pilot removed part of Erik's upper thigh and most of his left arm just as he hunched down over the bomb site, even while longing to wait and toggle his lethal freight into the Adriatic. One cannon shell, plus smoke and glass. It may as well have been ten.

Many nights after too much squash and too much gin I would restate my position. Not to brood. Never. Never. There was no way he might have hit the cathedral or even the imperial stables, since he couldn't hit a big green with a small ball—or a bag, for that matter. Probably even before the war. He shouldn't worry . . . but somber and glum Erik was. So much for the fiery humors of gin. It was a curse, and the colonel had then gone down into Ploesti's burning refineries.

Yes, that had been my last formal game. Such memories of a grand and noble romp turned jagged. I tossed more grass up into the Pacific coastal winds and mused, wondering how one could so clearly remember almost five decades later every minute, every stroke. We had played the second Yale nine first. As we strode toward the ninth tee, our last hole of eighteen, two huge pileated woodpeckers had drummed menacing early warnings through the swiftly darkening woods. I remembered . . . almost like Africa. Staccato, ominous signals. Not eagles at all. A much darker message.

Yale's ninth hole is a splendid architectural conception, but it can exude black Scottish wrath. In my estimation it really shouldn't be, as a hole, I mean. I was even then riding a pumped-up crest from my blast the week before at Merion, plus the intellectual glee of nailing the many facts in Hannibal's master stroke at Lake Trasimene. Of course, slings were used there, and spears rather than clubs. But here I was on one hot streak of energized golf. My last college game, and well below par for a change.

My partner, Erik, the One-Armed, was jubilant. At six over par he was one excited Norwegian son of Eli. Yet even pumped up now I could just sense some inner pull of fatigue from the tension of seventeen holes; and I was now two under par, very special on the Yale course. I sauntered toward the markers. "Why *not* a hole in one," my inner voice said, "to top off your years at old Eli?" My grand old dad, a teenage terror of Maine's links, would never believe it! Nor would any of my brothers, all of whom played better golf than I (not to mention my sisters). Would they believe it? But I had a witness along, an officer and a gentleman! Air Force, of course.

Yale's ninth resembles the ninth at Merion in that it is 185 short yards. But what a landscape, or more accurately, waterscape—a bleak Scottish tarn stretching from below the tee to a narrow apron girdling the yawning, two-tiered green. My long gaze now picked up this solid mass of liquid below me, which I had somehow never quite considered before. Whitecaps were suddenly kicking up on the dark water surface, challenging me. While hesitating, I still retained that mysterious "feel" vaunted by the peerless Bobby Jones. By Jove! God was in His heaven! Why *not* a hole in one to put me four under par for the eighteen? Yes! It might even be a record for the satanic links . . . such praise would be mine! I almost crowed inwardly. Psyched up. The distant woodpeckers drummed, but not for me. There was more afoot. A record!

The huge green is split midway by a deep velvet-like valley of hand-clipped grass, more chasm than trough. A ridiculous concept, halving the green like the berserk saber slash of a drunken dragoon. Tricky, yes, but just one of a hundred hazards the ninth boasts.

Little puffs of wind now whipped across the luxuriant tee. As I leaned over to thrust my wooden peg into the earth, it snapped into two pieces. The glorious "feel" suddenly left me. An omen, a portent! The once-fluttering flag was now stretched straight out, and very slowly it was veering around toward me. An Atlantic headwind was powering straight onshore across the bleak Long Island Sound. The pond below us now loomed larger, lake-like, beckoning.

It appeared suddenly worse than those hundreds of bunkers and traps called "The White Faces of Merion." In Pennsylvania, one had at least one chance to get out of the sand somehow; but this Connecticut lake was vast and deep, like the dark bogs of Beowulf. I gouged up a turf tee with my brown leather heel and soothed myself with Bobby Jones' explanation of "the feel." Why take practice swings when you're "on," when the rhythm is all coiled up inside bursting for release? But then, too, the Master had written much about balky headwinds—especially British links and seaside velocities. And that's where I was. Increasingly unsound beside Long Island Sound. Now faltering, I bagged my favorite three iron and yanked out a long steel-shafted two. Continuing in my deep and powerful backswing I reveled in the fatuous notion of "making a one with a two." So I lost concentration.

Yes, I did! My ball flew straight at the pin, but suddenly it paused and plopped down into the water, two yards short of the narrow apron. It may as well have been the English Channel. I was shocked. Thunderstruck. Very quickly I took out my persimmon wood spoon and then grimly splashed a second shot, lofting higher and falling even shorter than the first, and jinking off course, like a dove before number six shot.

"As you know, Erik," I said with shaky aplomb, "Harry Varden said, 'Whatever happens, never stop hitting the ball.'" With my brassie I accurately drove a somewhat scarred third Kro-Flite into the center of the pond. Then with my driver I savagely topped a fourth ball. It skittered down the front of the now hateful ninth tee into the tadpole depths. Crestfallen, or rather shattered at the total collapse of my game, I darkly stared with a slow-burning hatred across the consuming waters at the still virginal green. In kinder moments this is called loss of control, although I threw nothing. At age ten I was quite emphatically taught not to throw golf clubs. *Déclassé*, my father intoned.

"It takes balls to play golf," said my laconic partner, Erik, stoically. He rolled one over to my feet. Thinking of every champion of the past, especially the eccentricities of Leo Diegel, I then hit the fifth ball to the far end of the green. Staggering past the ruinous water I surveyed the green and took four putts to hole out. The rules in those days gave me a nine, as I remember it. (Fourteen today.) My last official eighteen holes of golf. I'm really sorry, Dad. The first two acts were great! It was a wet evening, that's for sure.

• • • •

But happily here I was on a special spring day in the Far West. There was no water around Firclad's verdant first fairway, and no onlookers. A thick stand of mixed conifers stood dead ahead down the sloping turf eighty-five or ninety yards. Best described as a copse. Part of the fairway was hidden from view, a long dogleg bearing off downhill, out of sight to the left. Above, an ocean breeze streaming up from the broad river's mouth was now carrying "my" soaring eagle toward a shaft of light over the broad ribbon of river on the mid-horizon. Not caring to take any practice swings with the pro's vision-enhanced eyes on me, I thought of fearless Ben Hogan in his forever memorable heroic clutch at Merion. "Strike hard and fair, and keep it brief," was Ben's motto.

Despite a gusting wind from the right my hard-hit ball rose from the tee, bent on a long trajectory over the forbidding copse; and to my long-disused golf eyes, truly out of sight! In one simple shot the Master's thoughts were released in a flood. Yes, I still knew the stance and how I thought I should look in a slow, full backswing; with total concentration of all power as my wrists cocked and the club head smashed the ball. Short and sweet. It was a Napoleonic concept. All power at one point. And what a sound! Solid! A sharp click. Better than any cricket bat and going more toward the famed Louisville Slugger, which George, the captain of our Yale nine, had so proudly flaunted years ago.

As I savored the moment, I heard the pro's far-off comment from the window. "Say, that's a caddie's swing if I ever saw one! You must have started playing when you were twelve." He was openly admiring.

"No, six," I responded with feeling, sponging up the praise. Who doesn't love compliments from a pro?

"You and Bobby Jones," said he. Was I pleased! He sure knew his golf trivia! "Don't ever change that swing," he added. Little did he know. It's the only one I have.

Some 265 yards down in a nice lush piece of rough grass I could just make out my ball, waiting quietly for my next idea; a tough downhill approach just over 190 yards to a marsh-lined green. It sloped off into an endless bed of skunk cabbage, still brilliant yellow. The cows of long ago must have loved number one. The baffie felt natural as a fishing rod in my hand, and the shot to be made was fully perceived in my mind as I strode toward the ball. Happily, the hillside behind me now screened the nice but nosy pro's view. I could again concentrate on my "very private person" re-entry game. What a spacious, unfettered feeling it was. Years seemed to drop away as I luxuriated, reflected, and then swiftly addressed the next shot. Relax, old man.

Then "click" went my ball. Oh so easy and so eager to travel. Fair into the wind with its luminous cloud background, but the baffie stroke seemed just a shade too hard. Out of sight! But then the ball dropped in the wind toward the flag and my eyes picked it up again, watching closely to see it roll off into the bog on the low side of the green. But no! It sank like a swallow into the sodden green and then moseyed three or four feet toward the cup. Carefully, I examined the dense green. But here . . . the greenskeeper pro reappeared again, up through his barbed wire fence from the boundary road below, to meet me on the green. He had me surrounded, and I hate onlookers.

"Is that your third shot?" he queried. Without thinking, I pulled out Alger's oversized mallet putter, a design I had always disdained over a blade, and quickly rapped my ball the few feet into the cup, circling halfway around the rim. Plop!

"No, that's my third . . . so I get a birdie" was my offhand response. Was I pleased? Yes. Stunned, rather.

"Not on this hole, buddy. If those are your shots, you've started your virgin round here with an eagle. Can you believe it? Wowie . . . ! Now listen, hang on a minute while I go get my clubs from my mowing machine parked just down there. I'd like to play the lower four holes with you, kind of show you the ropes." So much for being a very private person. But the gods were being truly generous—and far above us my eagle screamed, and I felt, with approval. What a re-entry! Now what to do . . . ?

THE SECOND HOLE

While my unwanted partner retrieved his clubs from his machine parked on the road below I tensely reviewed my mental state. So much, really, for my oh so very private person conceit. I had never planned to play with anyone. EVER. Mine was to be a forever solo game. The lonely prince, and winter rules at all times as well, plus second and third shots. Mulligans to the max.

The second tee just ahead looked less mangled than the brutalized first. The second hole layout in general appeared straightforward; a long, narrow, gradually rising incline, yet one not too demanding, except for the partially hidden green, sloping on either side down into wetlands. An immense native dogwood in full flower graced the upper edge of the green which I supposed must slope away from the middle crest. I had to assume; something I do not like to do. Only the top of the rippling red flag was in view just above the horizon line. Accuracy was the key here—no hooks and no fades. My attempts to relax failed. I was waiting on the pro. Tensions engulfed me. Tee off *now*. Speed was the solution. I impetuously unwound.

"What a shot! It's a perfect lie," said the pro, moving up to my side.

"It sure pays to slow down that backswing! Who would have believed those practice strokes . . . White lightning." Surely he had seen what really happened as he approached the tee. A normal person with reasonable vision would know and frankly look away with embarrassment.

His drive fell pleasantly short of mine by twenty yards. Somehow, however, it appeared to be just where he wanted it, maybe through long practice.

"Well, stranger, you've outdriven me on my own course."

"That may be, sir, but you may as well know I now lie three, thanks to those so-called 'practice swings.' It's best that you learn right now that those were clear misses . . . fans, we used to call them. That's the reason I very seldom take a planned practice swing near my ball. Then if I miss, it may look like something else, something more acceptable." I was thinking to myself, Tommy Armour be damned.

He was silent as we gradually walked up the long green slope. "I wondered—there's always that certain something about a whiff. But you know," he said brightly, "you look great even when you're missing." The flag was showing now, well above the hill line. A heavy belt of dark, ragged Douglas firs seemed to steady the green, anchoring the limerick green pool of grass. The dogwood, oversized at seventy feet plus, showed to beautiful advantage; all rich cream petals and red centers hanging above the green, which now revealed a deadly slope back, relentlessly down toward the far-off second tee. As usual, the hole was deceptive, basically backwards in some ways.

"What a curious approach," I offered. "It's almost like a military cannon shot on a reverse slope. Something from peninsular Spain."

"Thanks for that. I laid it out myself. The green is improperly masked, but there are no sand traps or surprises, unlike Wellington's day."

"Don't we lose our balls on the other side of the green?" I babbled. "That is, if I hit the green?" A brilliant sun burst from the scudding clouds. I could see that the dogwood was double-blossomed, shimmering in massive creamy grandeur. An "all-American piece," I noted with a native's pride. Concentrate! my brain signaled, slow and easy. You have the whole afternoon.

"The green had to be laid out just so because there's a sharp hillside rising beyond. And I couldn't give up that tree—it's known to every bird and man around. In the old days all the dairy cows rested under it, rain and shine." He drank in its glory like a country poet. Spring was obviously his season as well as mine.

"But here, maybe, just maybe, I can show you how it's done on this one." Very modest. He tapped a five iron precisely over the brow of the hill. With a little backspin, his ball lazed out of sight in line with the pin. From my vantage point I watched his ball just lip the cup, resting at last a few feet beyond. What an artist! And by the way, left-handed too, like Brueghel the Elder. Rather than fight all this it seemed smarter to turn it all into a free lesson from the most qualified guide, the course designer. But as Bismarck said of Queen Victoria, he "was making me schvett!"

"A local trick, and of course, I also place the cups," said my partner, smiling broadly. An unnecessary offering at best. But what fun that must afford him, especially since he had laid out the greens as well.

Practically closing my eyes and fervently praying for a hit, I lashed my ball fair into the middle of the beautiful dogwood. It was ingested without a sound by the earth-bound cloud.

"You were just right on distance," he calmly observed, "and maybe you'll have some luck." He couldn't know how grateful I was to have hit the ball at all. Observers paralyze me. But more to the point, the prospect! What a beautiful sight—the towering firs—their immense lambent branches, millions of needles rustling in the sun. The air was so gloriously, intoxicatingly fresh, blowing across thousands of Pacific Ocean miles from

Yedo or Cathay or some Spice Island. What a day! Try to relax, I again cautioned myself. Head down. Inch by inch.

Moving slowly over a hill so reminiscent of Wellington's favorite reverse ground against the French troops at Salamanca, I could see my new companion's ball. It was almost peering into the cup, having rolled down a bit more while I walked. He was a pro all right; I guess the only left-handed one I had ever seen. "The approach shots here are all in the wrists," he observed too modestly. Hmmm, was my silent reply. So often I've heard it. The wrists. All in the wrists. Roll those wrists. Cock them. Yes, yes . . . it always sounds so easy.

I surveyed the immense and drooping branches of dogwood blossoms. Well over a million, I ventured, and maybe half again. The new foliage was drenched in a billion crystal raindrops, more or less. A beautiful but deadly challenge for golf. As I skirted the vast base of spreading limbs, I spotted a line of huge, emphatic hoof prints emerging from the tree base. "Well, you said this used to be a cow pasture. It looks to me like they still feed here." But I looked again, and there in a deep cleft lay my ball, which must have bounced down off the sodden new leaves.

Who would believe, lying two strokes in a cow track, plus those two misses on the tee, of course? But I sallied, "What are the local rules on hoof prints?" The pro had his putter out and I thought he took a long time to size up and sink a putt I had already mentally given him.

"Let's have a look at your shot there," he said, striding across the shelving green. "I'll be damned. That's no cow, and you're in luck for sure. Your ball is sitting in a hoof print of Lucky Pierre's elk, our local legend. He's a big three-legged elk, as you probably saw."

No, I hadn't. I was thunderstruck. Who at Brookline would ever believe a story like this? The true prince of games even includes in its rule book for the deep prints of huge quadrupeds. "How I tracked the three-legged elk . . . and won!" Etc., etc. Something to dine out on, especially back East. Yes, an elk ate my ball. Or maybe it was a panther.

"You can see," the pro continued, "his hoof marks are really deep because he's supporting over nine hundred pounds on those three legs. And he's got antlers like a corporate hat rack, too. He's probably in velvet now. No doubt who it is. Old Lucky Pierre's elk is a local hero."

The rule he then enunciated was novel, surely unique. I could move my ball in any direction one club length, avoiding other hoof marks, deer, skunk, and coyote tracks included. One yard, that is, but no closer to the cup. This quirky local rule even so put me just on the lush apron. By Jove, I was in luck for sure and "the feel" was returning. Trying not to freeze, I stroked through and sent my new Titleist on a long curling journey toward the cup. Too fast, but very true. Thanks to the Great Golfer on high, it struck dead center and sank.

With élan, I fished my ball from the water-filled cup. Naturally I asked about Lucky Pierre's elk. "A somewhat unusual name," I ventured, "at least for an elk . . . anyway a three-legged one," I ended, somewhat lamely.

"Well, he's named for a guy in one of the old French-Canadian farm families around here, Pierre Violette, actually. His people ran the farm next to the Holstein dairy. The family goes way back to Hudson's Bay trapping times here on the lower river. If you know anything about voyageurs, that's what they were. When they retired from the Bay Company back then, they usually took to farming and fishing. Back in the late twenties and thirties . . . that's 1820, by the way."

"But of course," I added, a bit loftily. "The *coureurs des bois*."

"A few years ago old Pierre saw this young bull elk messing around with his Jerseys in the moonlight. That was no plan, even for a Frenchman.

THE SECOND HOLE

In the general excitement that night, he hit the elk on the left front leg with a broad-tipped arrow. I suppose coyotes took care of the rest of it, or maybe a cougar nipped the leg off. He's always identified now as Lucky Pierre's 'mascot.' Something of a local celebrity." This was the kind of story magazines are made of.

THE THIRD HOLE

S ilence overtook us as we walked the traverse toward the third tee, bordered with dense and dark salal in creamy blossom. Chunky cedar and spruce stumps from long ago rose from the verdant green, standing like husky, mysterious sentinels across the hillside, watchful reminders of a simpler age. In those days trees were something generally in the way and too big to think about.

"You know, if we're going to play the Great Game together, I'd better have an idea of your first name at least," I offered. A real, though halting advance from my low-profile stance. Was this a sign of improved mental health?

"Well, I don't use my real name around here, even on my bank papers. But if you won't tell, it's Tarquin. In return, I won't talk about your fast backswing. To believe it, a guy would have to see it, just to be certain. If one could, that is."

"It may be the reason I quit long ago, Quin. My swing usually had control of me, instead of the other way around."

"When was that?"

"Back in the late forties."

He looked back along the path to the undulating green of number two, weighing his words with some deliberation. "With a name like Tarquin McMurdo, I'm usually pretty careful what I say—but everything about your style and stance looks and says champion to me," he quirked, sensing some response.

"Well, Mac," liking that much better, "looks aren't enough in any circuit that I know about." He acknowledged Mac as "pretty much his regular name" as he briskly scrubbed his ball in the old-fashioned cleaner box. It seemed too early to indulge in reminiscence.

A distance off to the left of the oncoming third fairway, a majestic native maple appeared to be dropping its buds, thousands of them swirling in the afternoon sun. "Say, do maples drop their buds all at once here, Mac?"

"No. Wait until you're a bit closer and prepare for a rare sight. Those aren't buds. What you're really looking at is a huge swarm of yellow migrating goldfinches, thousands of them. They're moving north. Every year that tree is a favorite with them."

As I once more glanced back down toward the stately dogwood tree on the second green, I sensed some kind of movement low in the spreading branches. But it seemed that my eyes deceived me. The noble branches were moving *against* the breeze, and reams of blossoms were simply disappearing. A big appetite! So Lucky Pierre's elk may have been there all along! We had interrupted a late lunch deep inside the tree. Golf at the zoo! He was walking into the tree, not away from it.

"Counting just one 'practice swing,' you made par on two. But you really need to watch this third hole. The fairway's narrow, you see, and that salal is like a bottomless lake." I winced at that phrase.

"Now, my trick is to try and stay along the fairway and chip to the green—but if you're feeling reckless, go for a long drive straight to the green or the hill on its backside. Later in summer the hill is more dependable for a rollback on the green . . . and sometimes over and off. Far off." Experience spoke once again.

"How about the man I see mowing the green—what does he do?"

"Well, sometimes very little . . . that's my son, and he's watching every move we make. He's a fisherman, not a golfer. A hunter too, including searching for golf balls. Lots of them."

The operative word in all that exchange was "feeling," or maybe "feeling reckless." I drew out my long two iron.

"Why not a number two wood?" Mac queried.

"You mean a brassie?"

"Boy, does that date you! No one says 'brassie' or 'spoon' any more! We now go by the numbers." Frankly, I like the old names, the older the better, back to "mashie niblick" and "mid iron" times.

I examined the swirling bird mass, shot through with endless flashes of yellow speckle in the random sun. What a grand stroke to make. "I have no faith in brassies," was my calculated reply. "If I had thought more about this new bag of clubs, I would probably have left my number two, as you say, in the car . . . along with several others. So I'll follow your lead here."

"I'm trying out a new four wood, although it's metal," he stated, and with that his ball soared to the lip of the fairway, setting up a perfect pitch to the meandering green. He sensed my tension.

"Why don't you take a couple of practice strokes? . . . What I do is try to think about a very large full circle wrapping slowly around my body, like wrapping a medium-sized Christmas tree, taking lots of time."

THE THIRD HOLE

"How do you make a left-handed circle?" I quipped. But I knew instantly what he meant. More than fifty years before, I had first seen what appeared to be that perfect, articulated swing as drawn by the great Leonardo. He seemed to anticipate golf along with everything else.

. . . .

Yes. It was fifty years ago. No, more than that. I remember it was a Saturday morning, midway through the Great Depression. A man slowly pulled into the old country club parking lot, driving a medium-sized, highly polished blue coupe with white sidewalls. No one, but no one, played on Saturday morning during the Depression—especially in the mid-thirties.

As he got out, I saw that his wool shirt, sweater, and trousers were blue, and his bag and golf shoes were highly polished cordovan brown. And his face and hands were a leathery tan as well. Later I would come to realize that Beldon was truly his first name. He was an understated, totally orchestrated symphony.

Beldon Weeks always looked just like that—copenhagen blue and leathery brown, polished and burnished. A mysterious stranger—controlled, quiet, and elegant. In no time at all, our instantly deferential caddie master and then the pro had him lined up at the first tee. It was one of those moments. A solo player, just before the high-noon onrush of the managerial class to their private club—well, more or less private. Most unusual.

Greens fees were a dollar and a half then, all day. But you needed a reference to get on the course. The looks, the breeding—it counts. No problem there. Beldon exhibited the points, all of them. Silent, studious, intense blue eyes; courteous to a fault; no cursing, not audibly anyway. First-class equipment, too. Lots of gabardine. The right rain slicker. I spotted that. His practice swings were slow and thorough.

His driver was highly finished and the Honey Centers gleaming white spheres. His swing was graduated, very steady, fully articulated (although that wasn't the word I used then), and perfect for each shot. Grooved. I soon got his message—slow, steady, certain; and always the same. Calculated. Machine-tooled. Even to the last inch, a controlled total follow-through ending in a classic discus-thrower pose as his calm blue eyes followed the ball's predestined flight toward the flag. No apparent arthritis. No rheumatism or lumbago. Not yet. Driver, mid iron, mashie, it didn't matter. Beldon followed through; and as I soon learned, he made money at it. He was not a golf professional but a professional gambler on the links—on any course.

I was told much later that he had cut a wide swath through northern California and then the courses around Spokane (in Washington) on the summer circuit. Even—eeks!—Canada!

．．．．

I was thinking very hard about Beldon Weeks' long-ago swing as I sliced my two iron into the maple tree. The accursed concentration thing again.

An immense cloud of yellow, Ming yellow, and ebony jet heads exploded from all of the branches. My shot was more a powerful line drive fade bordering on a shank. But again the arboreal gods were kind. My ball calmed down at last. Disgorged, it nestled on the grass just inches in the rough. And one zillion bird swarms settled once more. But what a song they were singing. An astonishing reminder of Sir Joseph Banks and his

THE THIRD HOLE

first report on Australia. And again, I should have been thinking about my own swing, about my right-now problems, not Beldon's. No more day-dreaming. He was history after all, the past, the ancient period. Today's balls had to be struck today.

But at the time he had seemed like an ancient, solitary knight of some round table, maybe searching for the perfect golf course; always followed, I heard, by the card table, square or round—poker and, if asked, contract bridge. Nothing else. Nor could I figure it out when I at last learned that my classy knight errant was in fact on work days a disciplined, diligent fire extinguisher salesman. During the Depression it must have been a hard sell, especially during the long, wet winters our Pacific Northwest has always featured. Beldon at least did have a job, unlike so many. But he could not have lived on sales volume. His lifestyle was richly enhanced by golf and cards.

Of course we all wanted to caddie for him. He was undemanding, quiet and calm, resolute, and a good tipper; so long as you remained silent. Maybe a whole dollar for eighteen holes (including tip), unlike many rich players we caddied and shagged for. Some would curse horribly, cheat a bit here and there, and then quibble over a nickel tip. That's five cents, by the way.

Vernal sweatshops the courses were, but such a learning experience! Flying clubs were sometimes a genuine danger. But such an open window on the school of life. How intemperate some poor folks really are. On the playing field, that is . . . so long ago. Certainly not today. Not with television. Not in public, anyway.

"You weren't concentrating," said Mac. "Try to think of pausing just at the top of your backswing. Even if you don't think about it, *do* it. Really do it. Count to two. Focus!"

"Actually I was thinking about a golfer of long ago, Mac. Before your time. He used to play around here." Then I suddenly blurted out his name, to Mac's obvious astonishment.

"Beldon Weeks? Oh man, oh man, of course I knew him—old 'Beldon Blue,' the low-ball extinguisher. Boy, do you go back! I don't believe this! Little Boy Beldon! You'll have to explain all this, son."

We sauntered toward my lucky ball and the swirling mass of Ming yellow wings. I thought now about myself instead of Beldon and chipped my ball. It flew straight into the hopper of the mower moving along the green. "That's one I'm sure Mac's boy didn't anticipate," I murmured. A moving target.

"You are one hell of an interesting player. Real variety!" exclaimed Mac. "And now you cough up a name from California golf legends in the mid-thirties. . . . That's where I saw Beldon. He was a real money player, but somehow or other, he lacked the edge—or the points, as we say.

"I dropped out of high school in my junior year to be an assistant pro. And all the times he was around then, I didn't tumble to one fact. You see, Beldon never played for glory, only for money. I finally decided that maybe he didn't really like golf. It was more like a part-time job. Trophies and applause held no interest for Weeks, but dollars did." Mac pitched up next to the flag. "A southpaw phenomenon. Low ball and double or nothing. But what presence he had! A rare combination of grace and greed."

"You can certainly have that one," I said grandly, lining up my own impossible putt. His two-footer was in my way.

He suddenly looked somber. "No, I'll putt out. Years ago I decided always to putt through to the cup. Always." He had a very sloped, intense putting stance, most unusual to my mind. A crouch. Very low and eccentric, a Rodin pose.

THE THIRD HOLE

A survey of the impossible triple break I could plainly see left me uncertain and unsteady. "Never up, never in" was still my motto, yet I could feel no real sense of stroke. I recalled the incomparable Jones on overly long putts. "Never up, never in." I was disoriented; my mindset and many unused muscles were in disarray. The green had a hard, sandy appearance and my heavy-headed putter might drive the ball past the hole and then off the green. I had seen no practice putting green around Mac's "clubhouse." In fact there was no reasonable space for one. Boy, I need practice. Weeks of it. Oops! Here it would be all slope and I just had no sense of it. I realized that I had just taken a dozen or so putting strokes with no idea of where they might lead me.

"Never up, never in" is the motto around here," Mac opined. My far-too-comprehensive analysis complete, I stroked the ball. It lobbed along only a few stuttering feet. The green was strange, loathsomely slow, with countless wormholes. Near and yet so far. Even-handed as my stroke was, it contained no center of focused proximities.

Remembering Ernie Peepers' advice a half-century ago, I hunched down to re-examine the sun-filled green just once. A long rippling shadow splashed across the freshly cut grass around me. High above, a strangely silent ribbon of huge geese soared toward the north. "The first honkers," I exclaimed. "How beautiful."

"Yes, but they aren't geese. Late in the winter we always see some flocks of swan down in the river sloughs. You see that six- or seven-foot wingspread? Those are Trumpeters."

I thought about the jagged line they had descried across the green, another omen, and I tapped my ball along the imaginary line to the edge of the cup. "I like your idea, Mac. I will putt out too. It's really hard to miss a two-inch putt."

There was a long silence. I was now equating putting with muteness. ·
My partner seemed to tense only when he was around the cup.

Mac said, "Well, here's my son, Tan. Tan knows all the secrets of the
course."

"Nice meeting *you*, Tan. Could that be short for Tancred?"

There was a long silence and a deadly glance meaning yes! "Likewise.
And my lips are sealed. No one will ever learn that you attacked the endan-
gered goldfinches—all 39,000 of them. At least that was this morning's
count. And my mower, as well."

Mac's son was an easygoing wit, no doubt there. He engaged his dad in
some banter and general exchange. "I haven't cut number four green yet,
Dad. It's really wet and I thought you two might be pocking it up. You'll see
there's been a couple of big moles working uphill toward the green. They
look like sappers."

"We'll have to get them tonight. It will be a full moon. You know we're
hosting a team from the new upriver course Saturday noon. They'll probably be picky and moles are a no-no. Save some time."

"That's all I've heard about, picky picky. Some of our players—that is
to say your members, Dad, seem to be getting self-conscious and nervy. Not
all of them can hit a green, let alone my mowing machine." He shot me a
down-home look. Tancred would eventually get even with me in some offhand way, and not just once.

"Well, we've got a dark horse player here, Tan. He's playing right now
at one or two under par." Tan evinced mild interest, I thought.

"Well, I know it's not my skill," I muttered. "It must be your fairways,
not to mention your sound advice."

"Oh, well. The next hole will take care of that," said Tan. "I'm working
over the top five, Dad. They'll play well tomorrow if the weather holds."

THE THIRD HOLE

"My eternal optimist," said Mac. "This is real Scottish weather here. We expect a change maybe every ten minutes."

He shot a glance off toward the lonesome clubhouse and pulled a scorecard from his much-worn pockets to record our scores. Mac seemed lost in thought. Was it Beldon Weeks or me?

THE FOURTH HOLE

We approached number four tee over a low rise cloaked in wild clover. A distant hum came from several million honeybees working over the sweet carmine blossoms warmed by an occasional burst of urgent spring sun. Heady stuff.

There was no fairway in view, just a yawning chasm. A sullen mist seemed to waft off-center from its shadowy depths below the sun-drenched clover. On the far left side, masses of wild hazelnut trees tumbled down the dark abyss. Wagnerian possibilities here, I thought. Even a dragon or two. It was unsettling. Not for the hypertensive.

"This hole is called Indian's Revenge," said Mac. "And with good reason."

"I thought the Indians around here were peaceful," I ventured, "but perhaps guileful."

"Not so. This is a straightforward confrontation," Mac stated. "One of my devising, including the merciful bunker over there." I could easily see it, like a pendulous lip hanging below and half-surrounding the serene and untouched green. The conception was simple and yet perverse. Hit the green or the trap, otherwise forget it. The solution was too clear.

"That bunker has saved many a golfer's heart from bursting, and his balls from the pit below. Ladies included." Mac was savoring his cleft-like creation, a true alpine scramble. No, it was not for the faint-hearted.

But what excited my memory was the wooden bridge rising all along the right flank. A very extensive and utterly inviting bridge of long, unpeeled red alder logs and fancifully meshed and woven alder branches and twigs beckoned. The construction was a decorative, yet practical way to cross high and safely over the ravine below. Beguiling memories of my father flooded around me. Just such an artful bridge he had also erected long ago, with a cozy arbor and four benches midway along, somewhat reminiscent of the familiar Russian summer shelters known as "vodka huts," simple country structures drenched in memories of art and wood-craft and ardent spirits. In every sense the artful bridge was an eccentric regional architectural wonder.

"You know, I feel almost as though I have played this course before, certainly this hole—old number seven. Almost mirror-imaged."

"You do seem very much at home around here. I'll say that," observed Mac.

"Yes, but I'm talking about a course of sixty years ago, not far from here. Spanking new it was, and my dad was part-owner. It really seemed to us then as though he owned the mowers and tractor because he was running them all the time. Dawn to dark. Especially in spring."

"Sounds like the Big Depression to me."

"It sure was. Even bigger than the one I'm looking down into here. Anyway, there was one hole, old number seven, with a bridge like this and maybe as deep a pit. And it extracted revenge over and over. Does anyone ever climb down there, Tan?" I had engaged his interests again.

"Well, they send plenty of balls down there and—well, I clean it out every two weeks the way caddies used to do. It's pocket money, and the supply is dependable. Not many new balls though." He spoke like a philosophical realist. "The smart players usually choose a lesser brand off this tee. Something from the secondhand jar."

"The way *I* used to do, too," I replied. "Anyway, I've been gone a long time, but all of the stumps, salal, dandelions, and trees sure do remind me of my early days. And the bridge is English; it's right out of nineteenth-century Kent—say Strawberry Hill or some other English country retreat. Equally stylish, too."

"Or maybe eighteenth-century Cumberland," said Mac neatly.

"Well, maybe not *quite* that rustic," I rallied, "but we're on the same track. Something for the rural muses."

More mist wafted into the sun. A nice companion on the links, I mused. Mac was probably right at home with a bag full of hickory shafts and Walter Hagen balls. Was it only fifty years ago—well, fifty plus? Perhaps they were Tommy Armour's, his favorite whip staffs.

"So your father was a golfer," he prodded.

"Oh yes. An all-around golfer, just like you. He mowed the greens, clipped the aprons, and ran a fast tractor over the fairways, like six days a week. Lessons on Fridays. He wrapped clubs and varnished shafts with the best. Then he would always play eighteen in the afternoon. Right up until the morning of Pearl Harbor, that is. He canceled the rest of his game that Sunday . . . until August of 1945. Then he started right where he left off on the seventh fairway. On Sunday. Poetic."

"Sounds like I have a twin brother or fellow slave," Mac grunted. My eye followed the line of the bridge once again. Not the River Kwai, but rather a complete throwback to twig furniture on an American landscape scale—western and vast, that is. A two-way bridge yet. A true pleasure garden folly in "a wild and romantick valley, Cambrian Gothick in conception," and obviously Mac had built this too! Every kind of serrated fern snugged up against the tee and the bridge approaches. I could almost see my father's finely made tartan knickers heaving into view. "All work and no play makes a dull boy," Dad would say each Sunday. But how we all worked. And in memory, what grand play we had all together. Fly onward, time!

"I usually tap the ball with a spin," said Mac, expertly doing so. "The pin is sitting at about 160 yards." He completed the sentence and stood back. Serenity, thy name is Mac; there his ball rested, thirty-seven inches from the cup.

Skipping the practice stroke, my seven iron lofted the ball beautifully, but higher than anticipated, above the solid windbreak of trees backing the green. A sudden gust from the ocean caught its flight and dropped the ball on the lip of the green. It rolled effortlessly down into the bunker I had earnestly thought to put out of my mind. Was it concentration again or simply nature—the great betrayer? The Jones' sea wind . . . never forget its power. I obviously needed to review the Master's words, and better yet commit them to memory.

I could see the auburn head of Mac's son, Tan, now looming from behind a stump across the deep. "If you're in the bunker," he shouted across the void, "watch out for Indian remains."

What the devil? What an incentive, especially on a hole that shouldn't even be. From the crest of the green I could just see Tan working, obviously raking a shoulder-deep secret trap on the back side of the green. Maybe the front bunker was not second-best, since his trap, I later saw, was full of heavy beach sand and coarse pumice stone from the fiery volcanoes now lying dormant against the far eastern horizon. The bridge was a marvel, made for micturating, in the right circumstances, of course. Jones came back to mind, his usual practical self. The newly leafed trees made an aerial glade.

"Be sure to check the molehills, especially the new ones," Tan advised. Crossing Mac's bridge and scrambling down into the grassy bunker, I spotted my ball on the far side of a fresh row of dark earthen molehills marching across the heavy grass, just as reported. When I struck at the heavy mounds with my wedge, I wondered at Tan's curious advice. What on earth? Oops! There, suddenly in focus, two molehills ahead of my ball, lay a large and perfect obsidian Indian arrowhead resting on the wet earth. It glistened black in the sun, almost six inches long.

Except for Tan I never would have thought of such a thing—moles as archaeologists! Do the federal preservation laws temporize about this as well? Looking slyly about, I teed up, winter rules fashion, and with my particularly improved lie, blasted my ball up onto the green high above me. There in the earth ruins of my stroke lay another pair of less-imposing arrow points which I quickly pocketed for home analysis and cocktail rumination. What a spot for a golfing ethnographer. The molecular theory of archaeology . . . or was it gopherian?

In the interval, Mac had missed his long birdie, and he was waiting to putt a two-footer in for par. Again I said, "I'll give you that one." All in an offhand way from me. But he allowed as how we should both putt in. Quickly lining up a suddenly possible par, I could see the utter improbability of my lie, especially with the rough and pitted green running slaunch-wise some thirteen and a half feet between my ball and the cup. The fluttering shadow of the red flag was a further distraction, and though I always liked to have the flag in for approximate sighting purposes, I asked Mac to pull the pin. He did so with a narrow smile. Behind me the sound of coarse sand being raked faded away. Two spectators for the edgy private player. Bah!

With a smart tap my ball traveled in the sharp arc of an Indian bird-hunting bow. Just at the right moment, and following its own destiny, my Titleist slowed in mid-career and began to feel its own way down toward the cup. Slowly and purposefully my par was becoming reality. The ball almost dived for cover in the hole as I whooped in astonishment and relief. There would never be a repeat of that critical moment.

"Now how did you figure that one! That is very local knowledge," Mac said. "It is more than a hundred-to-one shot. More, even."

"It was a prayerful putt with its own Indian sign on it." With that, I showed off my surprising artifactual treasures to Tan and Mac. Tan himself had retrieved my ball from the cup. A silent compliment.

"Say, those are nice. What a find! Almost worth that curious afternoon side draft up from the Pacific. It puts the kibosh on most lofted shots."

"Now that's a great arrowhead. It's a special trade piece used for swans or elk," Tan continued.

"Why was it there in the bunker?" I queried. "It seemed so remote."

"Well, we think this canyon area was a kind of flyby. A rise of air follows up this long ravine behind us straight from the river banks. The dikes and the road and highway system naturally changed all the landscape down below, but climbing higher up, the draft is still here, just as it was in B.C."

"B.C.? You mean before . . . ?"

"I mean 'before civilization,' as we know it." His crooked grin followed. Lovers of landscape possess special charm.

"That's what caught your ball," offered Mac. "A real zephyr. Nothing like local knowledge in the land of the Western breeze."

"But how do you know that Indian hunters gathered here?"

"When we were making the course, here and there the chip piles alone were a sight to see. The early hunters would sit and work up these points while waiting for bird flights, or maybe elk or deer. That was before the time clock. What would you think of maybe two or three thousand years old? That's a lot of swan feathers."

"But where did this piece come from, and then these?" I said again, producing the others.

"The small ones are local, one is bone and one basalt," said Tan confidently. "But your trophy piece comes from down south maybe, from the Coos Bay area. The Coos Indians made big obsidian daggers and collected pileated woodpecker scalps. Great stylists, especially in war."

Tan was a fund of arcane knowledge. "Also, those points are found up north around Vancouver Island and even higher along the Inside Passage."

"To change subjects, you are also still one under par or so," said Mac. "This is one game I hate to leave, but here I go. If I don't get back to work, certain things won't happen tomorrow."

"And others will," chimed his son.

"But take this scorecard," said Mac. "You'll need it on the top five. Fill in your scores down here, just for my curiosity. Even a private person really ought to have a handicap, you know. We wouldn't post it. Not yet, anyway."

"Mac, I came into this world without one and I'd most like to leave the same way."

THE FOURTH HOLE

"Okay, then. Don't forget, we'd really like to have you on our members roster here at Firclad." With that warm expression to speed me up to the fifth tee, Mac was quickly out of sight.

THE FIFTH HOLE

He wouldn't know how strange it was that his fifth hole would bring back glorious memories. I recalled an afternoon at The Country Club at Brookline, Massachusetts, just as though it was a game played last week.

As I bent to my climb up to the fifth tee, the particulars of the legendary country club more than begged my consideration. Granted, the views in Massachusetts are more manicured and ordered. After all, the hallowed course considers itself to be the oldest south of Montreal. Number two in the Americas. And it is, perhaps. And not just golf alone—for the tireless, tennis and also world-class ice skating are offered, and swimming, too.

From Mac's towering fifth tee, a 295-degree cosmic view arced away over the tumultuous miles, an immense and still wild, as yet unfinished landscape, as so much of the West is. Disorder was the giant theme. Raw, unfinished, and not conducive to any casual measurements. At a grand distance downstream in the gray-green river channel below me, a huge battleship now emerged from a low-lying fog bank, making its ponderous way upriver to some cavernous naval drydock. How extraordinary. No views like this at The Country Club! Huge as it was, the ship looked tiny in this landscape. Everything did, except the mountains and the sun.

As we turned away from the fourth green, I looked back over the lip and down toward the quaint alder "gothick construction" while the past flooded over me and maybe through me once again. The feel of a similar fairway long ago was there all right, but also the sensation of another "top five," the very same idea of nine holes bifurcated by a sharply drawn landscape. It, too, was grand, raw, and unfinished; one already cut over by the first timber beasts pressing into the uncut Northwest forest landscape.

On they had marched—from the upper Mississippi to the Far West; timber cruisers and loggers from the Great Lakes and New Brunswick, from Maine, Michigan, Minnesota, and Wisconsin. Most often they were led by hard-driving Scots: the McDonalds, McPhails, McClintocks, McFaddens, MacTavishes, Wilsons, and McClellands; Thompsons, Bakers, Sterlings, Martins, Stewarts, and Hayes. An endless array of highland and lowland tribal names striding across the once endlessly wooded landscape of North America. And for them, the vanished forests of Britain, Germany, Finland, and Sweden just a distant memory. So, no wonder there were all the golf courses following behind the Brits and French-Canadians; rough and ready like their Scottish players. Those hearty Britons especially were always available for a strenuous afternoon in any kind of field sport, be it a white-water log drive or a deer, cricket, or bird-shoot. But in all weather and at all hours, golf. Golf was the passion.

As I recovered from the tortured pull up to the fifth tee, I realized that those childhood memories assailing me were not a little relentless. As I had pushed up the path, there seemed to be no way through the suddenly blooming wild violets which had forced themselves onto the trail. That was it! Their sweet scent lingered with me and again reminded me of less distant times; of a patch of hardy violets (or were they gentians?) near the seventeenth hole at the Brookline Club. Easter was late and spring was kind that last year in Massachusetts.

. . . .

The austere grandfather of a staunch college friend of mine, who had come back whole from Germany as a master sergeant in the dashing 82nd Airborne, had suddenly invited the two of us to play the famous eighteen. "His" eighteen. Although diffidently extended, Ned had exuberantly accepted his grandfather's invitation because he knew I would want to see the famous old layout. After all, guests were in those days, at best, tolerated.

The frosty old patriarch was ancient and crabbed, as was his game style. His was almost a three-piece-suit dress code. The tie was intact. I knew all the fine points of golf etiquette and manners, so we got on easily, if not famously—that is, until the celebrated seventeenth hole. The weather had been unseasonably humid, and as we left the sixteenth green, an intense warm breeze came boiling around against our backs, soaring along out of the curious approach road which at that point bisected the long fifteenth fairway nearby. I had walked along the verge of the path from the sixteenth green and thoughtlessly ground some just-blooming violets under my new cordovan golf shoes. Unfortunately, this caught frowning Mr. Gwynne's attention. It was later that I learned his true passion was wildflowers, not golf.

Nor in his icy reserve was he impressed with my mastery of several historical details of the young American star, Francis Ouimet's magnificent victory in 1913 on this very course. What a joy to look back on. Those incredible golf years before the Great Wars when the British were kings of the golf turf, and much more. I sensed that Grandfather Gwynne had never yet dealt with the rude fact that twenty-year-old Ouimet had formerly been a caddie around The Country Club, although one should mention right here that he was already the Bay State Champion prior to playing against the incomparable Vardon himself. His was an upset to savor through a lifetime, all of our lifetimes, for he earned such deep regard throughout his career.

I was getting the idea then that "Gramps" was still so stiff a patrician that even now he questioned some lapse in a system that had somehow allowed Ouimet to squirm through several Brahmin barriers. And then, not to mention some others, the incomparable likes of Walter Hagen, Gene Sarazen, plus other stalwart heroes with nerves of steel for upward mobility. I suppose he thought this change was good for America, maybe, but definitely not for Brookline. As if I were not breezy enough, the aforementioned spring wind was now funneling up a gale over our shoulders as I looked along the interesting dogleg of the storied seventeenth. A splendid *allée*.

"This is where one of our very own caddies won the American Open," murmured the still-perplexed patrician. "He defeated the greatest; imagine, he beating Vardon *and* Harry Ray!" His thin lips quivered. My amiable ex-staff-sergeant friend was looking over his arsenal of clubs while, I thought somewhat mulishly, turning over his grandfather's lofty remarks in his paratrooper's mind. He was fresh from the flattened ruins of Berlin and outskirts, and a quite different arrangement of bunkers loomed in his memory. Not to mention a shattered and contorted social system. The Back Bay approach might need an overhaul.

INCREDIBLE LIES

Not too far off, but just on the edge of our vision, I could just barely make out the seventeenth flag blowing straight back along the well-
topped green. One player could be seen standing just on the right-hand
apron. Gwynne's grandfather once again suddenly, yet sagely counseled
us from the historic past. "The day our caddie won the title he played
this fickle hole straight down the middle and then pitched to the green
with a mashie niblick."

A mashie niblick . . . yes, those *were* distant times. I had long favored
the mashie niblick, especially for its name. And yes, it certainly seemed a
most logical way to play the hole; but the hard wind was teasing my mind.
The Master had usually discussed the problems of a crosswind or shooting
into the wind; but here now was a grand following wind whose tempestu-
ous gusts would register maybe a seven plus on Beaufort's scale. Not down
around the grand old elm trunks surrounding us, but certainly higher up
along their new tops, where twigs and everything loose was being rapidly
trimmed away by the breeze.

At that point Ned Gwynne said to me, "Why don't you try my driving
iron? Someone has to break it in." I was curious and ready.

Who would believe a driving iron a unique club? Was this instantly part
of its attraction to me then? The swordsmen Roland and Oliver couldn't
have been more intrigued. A new weapon; and besides, I sensed "the feel"
coursing through me. Strike home, I thought. Just like Cyrano and other
great bladesmen. Somehow the number one felt longer, stronger even.

"The key here is to avoid the deep bunker," nattered Granddad.

I said in an offhand way, "My real concern in this wind are the players
on the green. It's embarrassing to shout 'fore!'"

His stately eyebrows raised like engineering marvels above icy eyes and
a thin smile. "Well, I think you'll be safe on that score." In one motion I

THE FIFTH HOLE

withdrew Ned's "number one" from his bag, drawing like Notung from the Wagnerian tree or Excalibur from the stone. How symbolic that I was shooting a Kro-Flite, because that was my intuition—to drive straight ahead just as the cunning bird flies!

A bit of tension entered my swing as I went through a speedy arc, and to my horror I more than just missed the ball. How agonizing! Gazing down the fairway as they were, my companions had obviously not noticed. Oh bravo! My incredible gaffe was simply accepted as the traditional practice swing. Oh, the luck of the gods who protect me! At the same time the now gale wind had blown my ball off its wood tee pick. "They're still on the green," said the old man with veiled sarcasm.

While he smirked, I reviewed my "feel," coupled with the sense of reigning champion Byron Nelson's latest advice on the backswing. "You must turn your shoulders as far as they will go," said that stalwart; and he had said it over and over again. And yes, moving my shoulders would slow down my backswing. Just so. I wondered if Gramps also remembered that Eddie Lowery was Ouimet's caddie that day. Ha!

My eyes actually saw the ball wing away from the club head with a sharp click. Reaching for the clear sky in a long gradual climb, my slightly hooked ball departed on a glorious unfettered journey. That was "the feel," all right. Effortless. Harmonious. Easy. Eddy Lowery was with me, flouting the Brahmin rules. My ball rounded deliberately and in a lazy hook, crossed high over the dogleg. Then I croaked, "Fore!" like a crow. "Fore, fore on seventeen," shouted Ned in a paratrooper's howl up into the wind. My Kro-Flite then meandered along the lip of the trap and rolled onto the green; but happily just below the pin and the players on the narrow sward above the flag.

"My God, boy! You shot into the foursome ahead of us!" exclaimed Gramps. He was looking even more pale and blue, except for two red dots on his down-East cheek bones. "It's never done. Never! Oh, my God. My first guests since the war!"

Mouth agape, he stalked ahead to apologize, tramping through a half-acre of helpless violets or gentians in his traumatized state. Ned hit a spoon to the approximate site of Ouimet's famous shots on the two rounds in 1913 when the seventeenth had then awarded him sweet victory over a shaken Vardon. We walked along together, lugging our bags, while Ned's gnarled grandfather hastened far ahead toward the green, followed by his engrossed caddie. We saw him suddenly slow down, approaching the seventeenth green with obvious reluctance.

"Oh my God," said sharp-eyed Ned. "Can you believe . . .! That's Frank Ouimet and the club pro, with their ancient caddies! They are talking about your shot. I wish we were up there now to hear the old governor explain your game plan." He chortled. Not me. "It's only a twosome, not a foursome," he snickered. Some twosome.

The men waved congenially to us and then turned to walk off toward the eighteenth tee, leaving our ancient partner to stare at my inert ball with still-disbelieving eyes and shaking mane.

"I'm terribly sorry I embarrassed our golfing party," said I, approaching the long and narrow green. "How could I have known my ball would carry so far?" I talked this up, with all the basic modesty and mewing sweetness in me welling up to full surge. "Just tell me what to do, sir." A humble utterance.

"Well, son, if you had to hit one of the shots of the century, what better place than in front of Frank Ouimet? Or should I say behind?" said

Gramps in a warmer mode. "Ouimet, that is to say Frank, said it was the shot he had always dreamed of." He fell to musing. I think he had forgotten that he never had played from the tee. We lined up our putts under his piercing eyes and I do not think that it pained him to see me then three-putt the famous hole. But I said, "The wind giveth and the wind bloweth away. Especially at force seven." And it is a wicked green the first time out. Of course he never invited me back. This probably had to do with the crushed wildflowers. *His* wildflowers.

All that weekend Grandpa the Glacial reviewed for one and all how I had driven into the great American master on his most famous hole . . . and then three-putted. He would slurp again from his rye and ginger ale, fully satisfied by both my prowess and my folly. Yes, golf is a splendid mystery, even less predictable than the players.

· · · ·

Here at Firclad, number five was an uneventful par plus one. I was bemused, but nonetheless remembered to record a bogie. So here the score stood at even par. And the winding path carried me along toward Firclad's sixth tee.

THE SIXTH HOLE

I savored the hues of bronzed vine maples arching and bending over the trail to the fairway, "crowding into a shade," as the inimitable Pope would have it. Among much else they seemed to screen a prodigious tree stump, extreme in its size, as though sent from another continent or planet. What a thought! Stumps of mystery.

My mind has always carried the odd idea, half-buried away with many others, that some day while hill-walking with my Life Partner, we would stumble on a long searched-for meteor, legendary, of record size. Yes, it would be huge, and when it was struck, it would give off a grand temple tone, as from a remote Chinese valley. We would identify a sound created in the heavens from which it had flown. Most likely we would stumble on it high up in an alpine meadow, well above timberline on a northeast flank. It would shimmer in the late autumn sun, radiating waves of mystery. One can always dream. One must.

When I at last struggled through the closely knit maple stalks I could make out the source of their nourishment—a humongous rotting cedar stump of a truly stupendous size. Had those first loggers who hacked and sawed to wrest such a tree to the ground seen it as a record-sized trophy, one of God's and nature's marvels? Raising my driver shaft to a horizontal, I could roughly estimate a diameter of fifteen to sixteen feet near the ground. Dia-meter, I say. A Herculean proportion planted by a deity. Nothing in Massachusetts would compare. Ever.

Underneath the sprawling roots I could just see a deep, shadowed cave, obviously the occasional lair of a big and highly pungent animal, or family of same. Squirrels and chipmunks had through many seasons sat on the freshly created stump some hundred years ago, and half-eaten seeds slithering down its gnarled bark had germinated through the years. In their special fashion, the coronet of vine maple leaves were already turning toward flame, scarlet red, and flame orange, even as they became green. A natural study in evanescence. The sun transformed it all into a shining emerald fairy house with shimmering interiors of reflected Vermeer yellow: an interior space designed somewhere in heaven, surely designed to drive some precious architects mad.

The sixth tee provided another grand view down toward the lower holes, and lower yet, the noble river lazed off to the west. The farmlands below appeared like "the fair fields of France," without their "order and tranquillity."

On the far hills above the opposite river bank, some five or six miles away, the depressing and emphatic effects of clear-cut forests were painfully evident. In fact the vast undulating panorama of hill and mountain slopes spread out a fifteen-mile example of the wisest and most wicked aspects of American forest practices, North and South. The stumps left by the earliest loggers stood as stolid century-old sentinels across the landscape, rising above the thick verdure around them like Martello towers. Wary fallers had long ago used their springboards to hoist themselves and their razor-honed axes up on the trunk to perch above the huge butts and the entangling jungle foliage of the forest floor. Strong, tireless, canny and crafty those axmen were, designed to live forever, arthritis and fevers excepted.

Elsewhere a planted, mature second-growth cut could be picked out, much of it still standing, waiting for the selected harvest of fifty- or sixty-year-old trees. These were grown in a sustained yield program, recognized by wise foresters as the only present and reasonable way to manage God's greatest plants. Spread along adjacent to them were the industrial wood lots with all manner of tree plantings at every stage of growth. Much of that was being erosively attacked by the vast physical dislocations caused by a severe, thousand-acre swath of recent and ruthless clear-cutting, rising nakedly above.

In that operation, all the squandered trees, from saplings to scions, had been brought low as though by a huge and remorseless scythe swinging up the steep hillsides in long and lethal strokes. Nothing had been replanted in the cut, and the ravaged landscape was laid out beneath the afternoon sun, raped and brutally raped again by greedy men—and by some others who were, of course, simply misled.

A deep-eating alluvial earth slide had vengefully removed the priceless topsoil built up through centuries to provide the forest feeding floor. Easily discerned ravines and the newly cut courses of runaway rivulets and "gully washers" had lacerated the hillside. Very recently, it appeared, hundreds and thousands of tons of earth and rocks had plummeted across alpine game trails, ancient Indian paths, roads and highways, railroads and ancient farmsteads. Gravity was king. Like big lacerating tentacles, slides which had already run their course had crashed far down into the river waters below, wiping out an elaborate salmon hatchery located in one of the countless creek inlets feeding the giant ocean-bound stream. Happily, most residences seemed to have survived.

Far down the slide, of which there would now obviously be many, swift currents of the Columbia River tried to carry the vast burden of earth and debris toward the Pacific. Several miles downstream a giant dredge from the U.S. Army Corps of Engineers coped day and night to keep the main shipping channel from silting up from the mindless despoiling of nature's bounty. Such a paradox. It all looked like the world's largest divot to me—but not one soon replaced. A true irony that the channel had to be kept open by government order to insure that foreign ships could dependably carry the logs stripped from the hills away to mills in far-off countries. Something was certainly out of kilter. No wonder Mother Nature was mad, for openers.

But closer to hand lay the interesting sixth fairway, which seemed to disappear over a moody horizon. After some solitary reflection, I selected my spoon—the three wood. Best to shoot toward what appeared to be the edge of a dogleg off to the right. No practice swing, just a smooth effortless stroke in the manner of Gene Sarazen. But no! What I produced was a sharp hook reminiscent of the young Hogan, well before the famous pro's rotating wrists theory took hold. A very long spoon shot, indeed one of my longest, but with a sharp tail I didn't need. I noted that far off, Tan had also followed the flight of my ball and even at that distance, across several fairways, I could see the shake of his head.

The brow of the horizon hill was bare of grass, in no way reminiscent of a fairway. This, of course, was the earth laid open by the first fallers and farmers and their tireless and close-eating cows, sheep, and goats. A long way from the luxuriant grass on the fairways of splendid Waverley far upstream.

. . . .

As I walked forward I had a sudden recollection of the crystalline dew-drenched green at Waverley on a June dawn at the height of "the season." A longtime friend had just made a hole in one (on the ninth) as the sun rose on Sunday, while still attired in his tuxedo and dancing pumps. And it was not his first! It was hardly fair. To think that he had danced all the night before and drunk not just a little bit.

In a reflective mode, my mind then bounced along to China somehow, its Tientsin port, and the barren fairways of the single course the old German colonial town on the north China coast had boasted. When World War II closed, my next older brother was stationed there with the 1st Reinforced Marine Division. As a fledgling ophthalmologist he served the Corps and definitely had his own eyes opened.

In 1947 there was still a functioning race track and bandstand near a lavish club, which the British had so wisely taken as part of their German spoils in World War I. The course was all dirt (China, of course, cut its forests down before the rest of us), but the clubhouse featured huge rooms, attentive twenty-four-hour service, an indoor swimming pool, pool tables, tennis—all the necessaries of those colonial days. And the retiring Japanese forces blew up fewer monuments than their German allies, especially nothing so rare as a golf course. And of course who knows what the future holds?

The traps were loose dirt and the greens were hard-rolled dirt; coolies were employed, constantly rolling each hard and level green. The scores after each round were recorded by scratches in the ground and carefully tended; especially since this occasion was the 1947 North China Open Championship.

. . . .

So I recalled this game of more than forty years ago while crossing the brow of the clay-clad slope of the sixth. No, the hole was not promising, certainly not aesthetically. Blind greens do not please me. The surprises are usually rude.

But as I crossed the brow an incredible change of scenery struck my eyes. Unlike the southern aspect, the north slope was all lush and green, unmanageably so. As I carefully scooted down the long, long grass, I pondered the possibilities of ever finding my ball. Ages ago in the days of depression golf, I had learned to follow the flight of every ball struck—like an eagle—which of course, meant six-power magnification. Some players would tip caddies properly for retrieving their frequent, erratic hooks and bad slices from the dense wet grasses and somber woods; but others would take our uncanny ferreting skill for granted. In such cases we would not always find their errant balls . . . but the present situation looked to me both impossible and joyful. My ball surely lurked in the immense and random wetland of magnificent and richly assorted wildflowers laid out below me.

A broad shaft of golden sunlight filtered through the heartwoods adjacent to the magnificent and unlooked-for display. It also posed a strange situation. The Firclad scorecard stated that there were no out-of-bounds here along the sixth unless one drove over the wire net fence running along the base of this left-hand slope. What a feast for the eye—a mass of yellows and whites running from *Lysichitum americanum* or skunk cabbage through *Sagiltaria cuneola* (arrowhead) or Arum-leaf wapato, *Sagiltaria latifolea* or Broadleaf Arrowhead Wapato, *Zigadenus venonsus* or Meadow-Death Camas, *Delphinium trollifolium* or Poison Larkspur, *Arunces sylvester* or Goat's beard, *Oplopanaxhorridum* or Devil's Club, and *Sanicula crassicaielis* or Western Snake Root, and many more. The wild array of unlike and intense colors blended perfectly. This was the ideal place for my plus fours or the knickers of fifty years ago, plus—garb still hanging in my sports closet. There *would* be a next time. The wild bed was a sodden mass and plus fours would have proved their practical design.

How could such a course of stunning surprises be longer kept secret? Did I somehow owe it to other players in other states and, for that matter, other countries to send out news of this galaxy of interesting, testing holes? I thought not. Not even a Grandpa Gwynne. Solitude, after all, is one of the evermore scarce luxuries. But I might reconsider. One likes to share within reason. Firclad and Mac were deserving.

As I plowed through the stunning floral parade, astonishing surprises were quickly revealed to my crafty niblick. The floral bed was also a mine of fine golf balls, almost like a riverbed of visual gold. Two Titleists, a Kro-Flight, Pinnacles, DS Fantoms, Top-Flite, XL Spaldings 1, 2, 3, and 4, Molitor, Pro Staff, U.S. Tigers, and others. But no Acushnets. Obviously with flush times, the art of retrieving good golf balls had fallen into disuse. Another example of conspicuous consumption and waste. But the curious problem was that my own ball seemed not to be among the round dozen I had uncovered. A golfer's dilemma on a moral plane . . . should I give myself a two-stroke penalty? But no. I was not out of bounds, in truth not even in the rough. Walter Hagen with his prodigious humor and sporting instinct about the lie of the ball would relish this "moral test of golf."

THE SIXTH HOLE

Reminiscent of "the great Haig" perhaps, I drew my mashie from the increasingly wet canvas bag and quickly clipped a Pinnacle onto the unseasonably hard green. Early as the season was, the grass there was turning dark brown, like peat. Such greens are referred to in Karachi as "chocolates," according to the world travelers in my family. Almost of necessity I took three putts to hole out, including the last which obstinately rolled once and a half around the imperious cup lip from two feet away.

THE SEVENTH HOLE

At last I stood on the seventh tee, a somewhat undistinguished rectangle of matted grass and awakening dandelion weeds. The sky to the southeast had taken on a dark and sullen cast. The hole was obviously a test of distance with a long, bending arc of fairway moving steadily out of view to the left, screened by serried alders. A hooker's dream, so long as the shot wasn't smothered. As I gauged the wind, probably force four on the Beaufort scale, a crashing sound in the same heavy, dark woods on the left caught my attention. In a series of astonishing leaps four lady elks now sailed uphill (!) over the high mesh fence, followed by Lucky Pierre's, who, for obvious reasons, plowed through the lost ball gate giving entry to the deep woods. In his enthusiasm he splintered one of the cedar posts holding the gate.

Directly in front of me the five immense animals loped across the fairway, bound, I instantly knew, for what had to be Lucky's lair beneath the great cedar stump. I knew in my heart that Hagen had never seen a performance like this, nor had any other ancient champion—not even in Ireland. Lucky's vast antlers compared with the spreading hat rack in the old Union Pacific Club. At least six perfect points, western-style almost and splendid, fully furred like the Irish stags of old.

He stepped daintily over my ball, which was still barely rolling along down the hillside. With an elegant bounce favoring his missing leg, Lucky then actually bugled toward me; not like Roland at Roncesvalles, but a deep-throated bell tone of the fully mature wapiti. He shot what was surely a leering look of the sated lord of creation in my direction, as he half-swooned and half-swaggered toward the sixth tee and his cows. I realized with a jolt that the four were all seriously pregnant, but unlike other bulls Lucky was still looking after his ladies fair. The heavenly bower on the sixth must be their "lying-in" hospital. How quickly they melded into the landscape. Their world, long before golf was dreamed of.

. . . .

My thoughts then lazily returned to China and Tientsin. So long ago. On the last fairway, playing for the "Nationalist Championship" plus a week's R&R in Japan, my hard-pressed brother later wrote to me that he could hear and see intense shellfire falling into the Communist positions on the perimeter. Down toward the sprawling city, clouds of smoke rose from the pounding Communist artillery, redistributing the rails and ties of the Tientsin-Peking line, along with assorted units of Chiang Kai-shek's regiments desperately holding onto the city. Across the final fairway occasional burps of automatic rifles, machine guns, and light mortar fire clotted up the atmosphere.

Even so the "greensmen" stoically strove to cosmeticize the final green, which was not yet pitted by hostile action. They rolled on, unperturbed. In golf, as in all great games, a bit of sangfroid is welcome. Ignoring all these lethal distractions, my brother Daniel had chalked up a 126 against the too-demanding hardpan course par established at 120.

"Big Jack," who captained an Ivy League team before the world blew up, slammed in at 128 in the same foursome, as a bullet splintered the flag staff in his unflappable caddie's grip. Such a finale! Shot and shell and the clash of ideologies!

. . . .

For sheer drama, Lucky Pierre's and his girlfriends could not hold a candle to the Chinese gambit. Theirs, however, was a great true-life experience, more lyrical and promising. And they sure pitted the fairway as well as the greens.

I trekked along the edge of the seventh fairway rough following an arc around to the left. The texture of the woods was rich and varied. Beyond the alders a series of very tall and straight firs, hemlocks, and wandering spruce formed a green texture—a Mortlake tapestry. The first in particular would have excited the interest and envy of any eighteenth-century sailor. A small forest of strong and straight, towering spars to refit any ship of the wooden fleets. Long, thin sun shafts falling through the murmuring tops and the long perpendicular lines of the shadowed trunks provided an Amiens Cathedral effect.

My ball continued to hide in the stubby wet sedge of the rough. From my granary of found balls I selected the Top Flight and helped myself to a nice mound of grass. While the green had not yet revealed itself to me, the topography suggested where it must be, continuing along to the left.

Since I was alone, two or three practice swings seemed appropriate, even though my energy was plainly flagging. On the top of my second swing a flicker of movement caught my eye. As I turned to confront whatever it might be, two long eagle feathers fluttered down through the branches to land near my golf bag. Yet another arresting omen. High up in the forest I could just make out a broken top on which a large aerie rested. I placed the sacred feathers inside my bag, transforming it into a sachem's bag for special enjoineries. Tomorrow I would bring my field glasses.

The surge of adrenaline stimulated by all these magical powers sent my Top Flight flying off toward the green. Upon rounding the bend I saw to my sorrow that Tan was standing on the green still 250 yards distant. My ball had clearly arrived as a surprise to him. But he was more than pleased to see the shot, which had traveled across the peat-like green to the dense apron beyond. With some concern for his scrutiny, my eighteen-foot chip shot still managed to roll along toward the flag. A tap in again provided an unlikely birdie (I was ignoring the lost ball for now) which must be magically linked to my soaring partner. Without comment Tan had moved up to the eighth tee.

THE EIGHTH HOLE

The eighth demanded another sharp climb in the Scottish hillside fashion, so I followed along. But now the miles of view to the south was in all ways sublime. It was a pleasure to see that Tan shared my sense of excitement in a stunning dimension of nature which was presented in spades. Even at that silent moment, an exceptional scene far below stopped my game plan reverie in mid-career. From a low bank of fog an immense military vessel slowly appeared, which gradually revealed itself as a vast battleship of the *Iowa* class. The last warship I had actually seen on this river was half a century earlier, the famous oak and pine U.S.S. *Constitution*, more familiar as "Old Ironsides" of 1812 fame.

"It's the U.S.S. *New Jersey*," announced Tan. "What a sight! She's at low throttle because of her draft in this channel. She's near bottom if not on it. You know those guns could carve some great bunkers up here for Dad's new nine holes or on any other course in a thirty-eight-mile diameter."

I could scarcely believe it. At this distance it appeared, if anything, more small than large simply because of the grand surround of nature. Yet Tan was right—the potential to overawe was far more transformed by the powerful damage it could do in a large diameter, hurling one-ton shells over God's landscape some eighteen radial miles or more.

"I find it all a bit hard to deal with, Tan. Along with all the other damage this behemoth can inflict, it has an atomic capacity."

"It's a mess," he said. "But it's a wondrous mess. I feel about it the way I do about old dinosaurs. If it turned out someone found a pod of such beasts, I would do everything to preserve them somewhere. Wouldn't you? And these big gunboats are some dinosaurs of our age."

"Ruskin once said 'a ship of the line may be God's greatest creation,'" I said a bit pompously. "What on earth would he say about these engineering marvels and the men who created them and the men—and now some women—who make them go." Titanic, majestic, and in all ways impressive monarchs of the deep.

The lumbering warship glided around a point of land into a curling mist, its whistle intoning an imperious warning upstream. I turned away from the scene and slashed a hard, straight nine iron into the front of the minute eighth green. Another good shot! When I reached the small crest of the short fairway a painful surprise was revealed. As might be expected, a small but very deep, seldom-raked trap protected the green. Bad news. It was more pit than sand trap. The sands of Nakajima. No place for the unsteady of wind and limb.

I sorted through Alger's gift bag and found his heavy wedge, a new club unknown to me, although its employment was obvious. I have never truly mastered nor understood the art of pitching out of a sand trap. In early years I had very good luck avoiding them. The blunt fact was that I had always enjoyed playing golf, not practicing golf. Beldon was the first person I ever saw, other than our local pro, who actually practiced shots. Of course that was all before the attraction of driving ranges, but even those curious installations don't feature trap practice. Not even in Japan. Beldon's easy stance came back to me. The perfect circle. Then I drew deep on family lore. But it was unavailing.

Such a time I had in the trap. Mercifully, it was a solitary adventure—unobserved. Entering the trap maybe two under par, I emerged from the pit three over. Another humbling experience (and punishment for my faulty addition on seven). The episode should have brought me to my knees just from sheer fatigue. Speaking of which, this very private player suddenly sensed an even further drop of energy. After all, I had not walked around a course in many years, and Firclad was maybe more Welsh hill farm than American luxury golfing. Nor had I ever packed so many clubs. I had counted them now several times. There were redundancies, not to mention my imposing addition of years.

As I searched for the sequestered ninth tee my eye picked up a swirling skein of swans madly careening about on the far-off horizon. They were caught in a line squall which seemed to be moving upriver out of the notoriously fickle Pacific. It was a glorious nineteenth-century aspect. Caspar Friedrich would have called it his own.

THE EIGHTH HOLE

THE NINTH HOLE

A n absolutely immense field of Lincoln green ferns stood along the hillock above the dastardly eighth, and the ninth tee seemed to be lurking just there. When I reached the tee markers, they appropriately pointed due west. I could see another very long, hidden hole. My downfall—the sunken road at Waterloo came to mind.

It seemed very straightforward in its way, but bisected by ridges that screened any view of a well-struck ball's flight and descent. As I savored the distant view and studied my immediate golf problem, Mac arrived with a clatter. With wonderful élan he once more sprang from the tractor seat and bounded up the slope toward me. He was almost prancing, and this at seventy-two plus. I was not. I surely needed some restorative, preferably a two-ounce bolt of Rémy—or any cognac, for that matter. Even brandy.

"How did it go on the eighth?" he asked.

Morose, I eyed him silently. "The fact is I've saved myself for the ninth." No point in mentioning the pit of despair. I spotted the swans beginning to circle.

"We have a peculiar kind of local wind coming straight for us, but it's going to change direction fast and hard."

"Will it be at my back then?"

"Yes, but with all these big trees around you might rather just come over to the clubhouse now." Mac squinted hard across the fir-covered hillside. For the first time some concern clouded his merry features.

"Well, I can't resist some help so I'll wait a few minutes, Mac. The wind will push my drive along, and my aching body as well."

"Okay, but watch for falling trees. If you're going to become a member of Firclad I don't want to lose you before we get your check signed."

He rolled his tractor over the first hill and careened out of sight, just as a fierce blast of wind bent the trees above and struck me on the left quarter. It was more than Beaufort's force six ("a strong breeze"), more force seven ("a moderate gale" with "whole trees in motion"— which they were, and even more). Increasing velocity powered swiftly through the "twigs breaking off trees" of the "fresh gale" at eight to force nine: "a strong gale." I noted the somewhat ramshackle cedar shake roof over the old water tower; it cracked and suddenly disassembled like a big clutch of crows. Old cedar shingles flew in all directions. Had there been "chimney pots and slates" at hand as described by the famous Francis Beaufort, Admiral of the Red, they would have been "removed along with other structural damage." It was a howler laced with occasional shrieks and moans.

I was, of course, entranced. My practice swing followed through with a snap, but the simple fact was I could not keep my ball up on the tee long enough to drive it west. A small grove of nearby elongated firs was then uprooted and crashed in a tangle below the tee. Firs are notoriously shallow-rooted, but still the winds must now be approaching force ten, "a whole gale." Even so, I kicked up an earth tee with my heel and cracked a perfectly marvelous drive straight out of sight, right down the center line

THE NINTH HOLE

of the beckoning fairway now lashed by trees on either side. My ball rode the crest of the gales. Such an adventure, and me with no windbreaker.

The soughing wind jogged my memory. Years earlier my wonderful walking companion through life had bounced around a unique course with me, one overlooking Scapa Flow in the Orkneys. What a walk to remember, but much safer. The forests were long gone from these fabled islands. Not a tree in sight to be uprooted or thinned of its twigs and branches. And now here was another elemental day to remember as I half-ran and half-staggered across the hillside. Such a splintering noise! Down went the trees.

Later Mac declared, "I could hardly believe what happened then. I'd just come in the shop and was having my 'elevenses,' late as it was. There was a sharp knock and the ball you drove actually struck the wall next to my window. Then it bounced off and rolled down onto the green, rolling directly to the flag."

He warmed to his story. "But then, by golly, the wind got behind it and pushed it over the short lip of the green, down forward into the blackberry ravine. I know that you were lying one. Do you know that you almost had a forever Guinness record hole in one . . . at 436 yards?" He fixed me with a glittering eye. "While I was worrying about what to tell you, a big tree our greens committee has been fighting about for more than ten years fell over right on top of the whole scene." His glass was raised high, eyes very wide and blue. "Your ball is under it somewhere, I think."

"Well, I earlier decided to play for plain old pleasure, Mac. Shots, not score. At my age I can kiss scratch play farewell without a murmur." I could blithely lie with the best of them. No point in mentioning my score on the eighth. One can be too erratic. Tan had no doubt witnessed my collapse.

And, I added unnecessarily, "It's not the score anyway, but the pure pleasure of an occasional shot." I struck this dead horse once more with real feeling. The wind raged.

Mac loyally supported me. "During the Depression I used to play with a guy who would hunt thirty or forty minutes for a ball in the woods. Foursomes would play through us. Ladies foursomes! And he would say, 'It's not the ball, it's the principle of the damn thing. . . . And besides,' he would then add, 'it was a new ball.' Out of every four hours he dependably spent one and a half in the woods." Mac was shouting in the gale.

"He must have slowed down your game."

"Well, I hung onto him long enough to unlock something of his secret of putting. He was a lefty too. Then I willed him to a like-minded ball hunter."

"Well, I've seen everything today, starting out with a most agreeable introduction to what is now my favorite course, to which I'll toast in a drink or two and then be on my way. Mac, I'm pooped!"

"Oh no, my young friend. As soon as this vagrant wind moves off we must go out and finish your round. That's part of the whole follow-through. The mystique. You must hole out. Long ago a great player said 'never stop hitting the ball.'"

"Harry Vardon. The Jersey Wonder."

"The very one."

"He was a study in steadiness."

"Not like the Master, but very steady, studiedly so."

"But not the legendary putter, not on our American greens anyway." We each lapsed into memory. Great putters are harder to remember than long drivers. It should really be the other way around. The great crunch is around the cup, close in.

THE NINTH HOLE

The wind continued in full sway, sucking random red cedar shingles from Mac's rustic social center. Mac's nourishment was gone so we settled down with a few pegs taken from the flask I ever carry in a poacher's pocket.

"So you were going to tell me a story about finishing out each hole." My curiosity was overwhelming my manners.

"So then, you noticed," said Mac idly.

"Well, on the second green I had a feeling you had seen a bit more than I ever would." That moved him just a bit, as he savored my Rémy, slowly reaching a big decision. He achieved closure and launched into the story.

"I'll admit to having one great season. Real days of glory stuff. But you know, that was a long time ago, and nobody made any real money then, not to speak of, anyway." He sniffed the dark amber essence and took heart. He rolled the Rémy around his tongue.

"For some reason I suddenly took off—not so much with the woods but my irons. I was in a trance, a kind of iron-thinking euphoria. It was 1935. Some guys groused about my occult charms and spells. A bloody left-handed magician. My short game was a study in back spins and the art of necromancy, but it all seemed natural skill to me. Not luck, just the natural way of things.

"Of about twenty eagles I shot that one summer, most of them backed into the hole on spin. That's what really got to them—backing into the cup. Let's be frank, twenty-two eagles. I remember each one, minute by minute, rain and shine: The Olympic, Cypress, Pebble Beach, San José.

"One day with Ernie Pieper, I racked up two eagles. He never forgot. Ernie said, 'You could be a left-handed Bobby Jones,' whatever the hell that meant. He knew no one could touch Jones, although laconic Ernie had given it a real sportsman's try; so naturally I was flattered."

"Seems to me Ernie spooked the Master a couple of times down in California." Even I remember that. But Mac was on a roll now.

"I was playing so well, as I said, I stopped thinking about it."

"That sounds good, but I don't think that works in this particular game. Somehow, Mac, the inner self can never become an observer of golf. There always has to be a personal involvement with one's own game. Call it what you will."

"That's a good thought," Mac chimed. "You know. . . that could be what finally happened to me in the L.A. Open. I was the medalist in the qualifying round. They still remember my score. It's still the course record. But then the next day I ended up being an observer."

"What do you mean? Were you *disqualified*?"

"Oh no. It was a thirty-six-hole tournament, and I was playing my best game of the whole season. I'd already made enough money to buy a green V-8 with side walls, an engagement ring, and lay away a new set of irons. It seemed like I could do no wrong that final day, even though the wind was blowing sixty across Santa Monica. It's hard to believe now. On the eighteenth I was eight under; and you know, in those days, half my clubs were hickory shafts! I was already nicknamed 'the southern wonder.'"

He was still warming up to a long pent-up story of long ago. And left-handed, too.

"And the rules weren't so complex as now. I had chipped in so close to the cup I had to lift my ball for the other three of my foursome, one of whom was playing his last Open. He was six under. I could see that, but my caddie knew the tournament was mine."

"It was awful bad luck . . . talk about spells. My caddie simply said 'Hot dog! Congrats.' I said, 'Thanks. Boy, did I need this one.' The shadows were really long and the wind was flapping our pant legs. You know that can be

THE NINTH HOLE

distracting. The other players holed out and, probably overwhelmed with relief, I walked toward the clubhouse to turn in my score at eight under." He lapsed into silence.

"You mean . . . are you saying that you forgot to put your ball down . . . to putt out?" "Incredulous" hardly covered my reaction.

"I didn't tap in. I had put the bloody ball in my pocket and mentally checked out. Then I walked toward the locker room. This was long before TV, you know. Everyone was just standing around the green watching."

I gasped, "But then . . . you were *disqualified*!!"

He nodded morosely. "Those were the rules. Everyone was simply staring at me in shock. So you see, ever since then I've holed out every putt, two feet or two inches. I never won a big tournament after that, either. That was my green flash. When people looked at me later they were always embarrassed and bewildered. So was I. What a goof it was! For me, golf became one long wake until the war came."

With that painful close to his tale we finished my godly essence and spoke no more; but neither would I ever forget. Now I was looking sad and morose. His eyes were glittering like "an ancient golfer." One minute of inattention in a game that is all focus from one's waking moment . . .

Finally it was time to go. The wind had died, the Rémy was gone, and a chill was coursing through the new chinks in Mac's snuggery—now my favorite western clubhouse. But Mac was having none of my sympathetic murmurings. "Hey, get your nine iron out and follow me," he ordered.

So down the slope we clambered, across the ninth green. It seemed a miniaturized version of my inglorious ninth at Yale. Over the lip and down the steep-approach slope. My ball was hiding in a great mass of fallen and fractured limbs.

"Now, by every standard you were in the fairway until golf's merciless god felled a tree into your game plan. Drop a ball here, son," he said. "This is my course after all, and I still make the rules."

"I didn't bring one down," said I, on the point of whining from muscle seizures. Mac could call me "son" if he chose, since everything else seemed unreal.

"I'm sure someone has, through the years, reminded you that it takes balls to play golf," said he sternly, rolling a Kro-Flite toward me. "I'll run up and give you a line on the pin." And at seventy-two, that's what he did—speeding straight uphill, just like Lucky Pierre's. So who said the legs go first? They're wrong, anyway.

Trying to do just right with a niblick calls for more finesse than I've had in forty years. But somehow I caught the Kro-Flite just right (no practice swing). It rose above Mac in the dusk, too strong, but dead on line, thanks to Rémy and a sense of resolution.

There was a long silence on the verge above me. Mac's head appeared at the brim. "Your ball is right next to the hole. Three inches. It backed in from about eight feet."

"You mean I get a birdie?"

"No, Mr. Scratch, you began and ended my sporty nine with an eagle! What will the other members think of this crazy story?"

"If we don't tell them, we won't have to worry. All I know this minute is I'm too tired to climb back up the hill to where you are. But you can see I sure was listening to your story. Backspin is my new motto!"

As I slowly made my way up the slope I looked far off beyond my special Tarpeian rock, now the first tee. Was I hearing just the faintest screech? Had the great eagle of Firclad witnessed my astounding re-entry into the

THE NINTH HOLE

arcane mysteries of earth's greatest solo game? Was it the sound of approval—exultant approval—or disbelief?

As I slowly moved off toward my car I glanced through the snuggery window. Mac was poring over a score card. He had kept his own card on my play—probably with Tan's help. His head was shaking in wonderment, one that I gladly shared.

AN INTERLUDE

As I drove downstream to our newly found river house, an immense cloud of eddying Canada and snow geese settled slowly, drifting from the cobalt sky into the dusky fields around me. Deer were gliding through the shadows, down to the shrouded river bank for a bellyful of cool water. I drove carefully and thought about all the wonderment of the color green, and all its shades that I had seen this day: verdigris, celadon, bice and Lincoln, berylline and Brewster green, virescent and apple, peridot and jasper, forest and garden green, chalcedon and aquamarine and splendid malachite. I thought of the green of the grass and the emerald green of my walking partner's eyes. What a prospect life was.

I would build a fire and we would look off toward Cathay. We would have a very friendly drink, or maybe two. Her eyes would glow as I reported on my newfound earthly treasures, Firclad and Mac. Some giggles. No doubt about that. Maybe a guffaw, even.

I awoke in the morning thinking of duck egg green. And what a misty sight from our windows as geese in their honking thousands flapped past our windows. seeking altitude for their flights to the farmers' fields. Yesterday could easily have been a dream were it not for a small blister on my right thumb and a grand ache in all bones. It was serious enough to make me think of horse liniment. Anything to ease the joints and gears.

In a melee of flotsam brought in on the nine-foot morning tide, I could just make out a sizable flock of red-headed mergansers surging and diving beneath the flaring mists. Two haughty blue herons stood stoically regarding each other's feathered charms between quick gulps of fleshy bullhead. Wood ducks rode the surge, swelling into the rotting pilings from the wake of a wondrously orange-painted, deep-laden wheat carrier a long two iron off in the river channel. What a morning! But oh, how stiff I was. My hands, my back, especially low down, and my feet, oh, oh, oh! Is this the onset of the evening of life as some smarmy life insurers say? Now, just when I have redis-covered the great game, one demanding all one's craft, one's strength and skill—every atom of inner discipline? I drew our large bath and examined the downstream traffic. No battleship today. My joints gave thanks for the steamy, neck-deep water. Hot water, an ancient luxury. Very Roman.

I reflected. Just a few weeks earlier a Chinese colleague and friend of forty years had stopped by our city house on a visit from Beijing. We all talked of a thousand unbelievable things which had occurred since our last meeting. Then he opined of our life, "To retire at the height of one's pow-ers is Heaven's way."

I had then quaffed so noble an observation from ancient China, but now this morning I was not so sure. I may have more than passed the height of my physical powers. I soliloquized. My great partner in all things now agreed, but with novel and reassuring reservations. It was a Turneresque morning for savoring, not mewing over inventories of aches and sprains.

From the number of seal heads I could see breaking the river surface, the spring salmon run must be coming on. There is simply nothing sweeter and finer than a well-fed spring Chinook, as every seal would attest. They like a big belly of eggs, 6,000 potential salmon. Golf would have to wait while we trolled the tide pool below our newly discovered house; and just perhaps fire a 12-gauge slug or two into the misty trees where a cloud of raucous crows were nesting and squawking about territorial rights and privileges.

But in the meantime one could review the events of yesterday amidst the deep swirl of steamy soft bath water and colored recollections. Could Firclad really have been so fine? Did it all really happen? My mind questioned, but my body again groaned. Yes, a bruised champion, but I had scored three under . . . more or less . . . the eighth hole mercifully set aside.

• • • •

I was intrigued by streams of recollection, fishing as it were in Thoreau's river of time. My mother was one of the unsung Western horsewomen of the early twentieth century, performing in the first Calgary Stampede and riding across Gunsite Pass as a girl. And yet through some geographical quirk she and her several sisters had also been introduced to golf by my errant Celtic grandfather. He had laid out a rough and rude but glorious five holes in his craggy landscape, now incorporated within Glacier National Park. My maternal grandfather had played the game across in Wales and Ireland before his parents summarily dispatched him over the Atlantic in the 1840s; just ahead of, I'm told, the agents of some part of Her Majesty's too elaborate and nosy customs hierarchy. We all longed to see the copybook he had so grandly blotted. Some day, perhaps.

When my father came west on his first transcontinental outing from Portland, Maine, the Browne girls of Montana were more than equipped to talk golf; especially the wonders of the splendid Curtis sisters, Harriet and Margaret, dragging their heavy golfing skirts and clubs around far-off Brookline and other Eastern clubs. And my father surely embroidered on the New England theme—international golf. He knew its lineage like the stud book of another turf sport. The fierce competitiveness of Beatrix Hoyt playing out of Southampton's Shinnecock Hills and the stylish mashie shots of Frances Griscom. The lissome flair of Ruth Underhill as she cut her opponents down in the last national championship of the nineteenth century had especially impressed my mother.

Was that my father's courting cue? Had he *really* known Ruth? Who's to say. . . . What Kit had taken as her own was the very full Underhill swing plus the nerveless concentration—and Miss Browne also took my father in hand at full gallop; his devotion to the links prowess of Mrs. Caleb Fox and the early powerhouse Gertrude Fiske notwithstanding.

I took a special delight in the thought of how astonished my mother would be, me, the least-skilled of her golfing brood now suddenly coming to flower in the sunset of the century. A later and short bloomer, but maybe memorable. My older sister had also continued my parent's steady admiration for the long and tenacious links career of Mrs. Caleb Fox of Philadelphia. But somehow my sisters, Kathleen and Mary, were smitten most by the great amateur Glenna Collett; or it may have been the high style photograph of Collett Vare playing in the first Curtis Cup that swept them away; that until the modernist Patty Berg came along. What a very grand champion she was, and one they naturally bonded with, accepting her style and sporting instincts without question. Such dashing times they were. That, too, was heaven's way. A very fond look backward to the height of certain powers. And now it seemed an innocent time.

• • • •

I was painfully aware—yes that's the precise word—most sensitive to the fact that I had played a lot of golf in one short day. A couple of fingers and one ankle, broken more than once in far distant soccer fields, reminded me not only of the rush of seasons; but even more of late that each year now seemed to sprint. But how happily I remembered them all, barring a few jarring details. I turned on the Jacuzzi. Ahhh, yes.

Our breakfast was noble, especially the café au lait followed by one café royale, but salmon on a flood tide don't wait around for breakfast luxuriating. I quickly sharpened two hooks attached to my oldest bronze reel on a six-foot boat rod and listened to my Life Partner expound on food. Using great gobs of red salmon eggs for bait was somehow a waste, she proclaimed. As well, she had views on the attractions of women's golf at the end of the nineteenth century.

These L.P. now gave while neatly guiding our large skiff down through banks of mist clinging to the ragged pilings of a long-vanished lumber mill; one which had cut mammoth bridge timbers for the railroads between Shanghai, Harbin, Vladivostok, and Baikal. Despite the tremendous military forays through that vast Far Eastern geography, several of the timber spans still served the Russian rail lines ninety years later. So much for the quality of Douglas fir.

As we slid by a huge, half-submerged cedar log, L.P. commented on those stylish women of old who anticipated and savored the same sense of release as male players, smartly stepping off a first tee on yet another journey into the unknown. She skillfully shipped one oar as we raced by the ten-foot cedar butt ponderously bobbing like a hippo in the strong race.

AN INTERLUDE

Just as dangerous, too. Two red-throated loons surfaced in surprise, gazing on L.P. almost as a regular friend familiar to their mysterious eyes. What had they seen on their predatory submarine journey?

There is no doubt, loons are unlike all other marvelous birds. Theirs is a different world, deeper, darker, and more cosmic, yes; but somber? No. L.P. and our youngest daughter expertly imitate the cry of the loons, an eerie sound only when they respond from a far-away shadow in the first darkening of sunset. My feeble attempt is always identified as the yellow-bellied loon, a species yet to be recorded by Petersen.

Mulling it over in my usual sense of inner wonderment, I then settled on an expertly filleted herring half, attached to a more than antique #5 flasher. I sent the rig off into the edge of a tide race where a seal had shown his shiny head three minutes earlier. They always know where the best fish are, drat them.

One of my more clever readers of river water had generously pointed out the prospects of a sub-surface ledge about here. A basalt ledge provided a rest stop for larger Chinook slowly working their way upstream in the deep waters running just below the palisaded hillside. Moving, holding, moving, and resting, conserving everything for the daunting journey home.

As I turned to check for freighter sounds in the mist upstream, the stout rod was almost torn from my hands. We weren't ready for that! I certainly wasn't. Heavy line raced from the whining spool. The brake hadn't even been set right. An obviously huge Chinook was already out of sight in the fog on the opposite bank of our stream; a long point of heavy sand with tide waves rolling over it from the Columbia. I could feel him chewing and crunching the big hook. Fortunately I had used a long piece of wire leader, a local procedure I try to remember with the big, sweet, and meaty "June hogs." Such a name for so noble a member of Pope's "finny tribe." A line of low-flying geese sped overhead, cackling their alarm at our appearance in their secret universe. There was too much happening too soon. I was actually uneasy and curiously awkward in the face of this powerful hit; too many lines, gaffs, nets, and extra gear fouling the floorboards. And tides are remorseless.

With rude surprise the upstream fog was rent by a blasting ship's whistle—chillingly close! With radar to aid them, freighters moved purposely through dark nights, snow, fog, or blinding rain. And fast. This one was bearing down on us blind and upstream. Or so I thought.

Not wasting a moment, L.P. put the little Sea Gull outboard motor in an operating mode and got our dependable British pusher running. She turned the skiff quickly back into our tiny stream with an uncanny sense of our precise location in the turbulent water. The cause of our unease, a salmon of heroic proportions, had turned meanwhile, and was moving back across the stream toward our skiff. I furiously reeled the line in—dripping reams of it.

Trying to cope with cold water and finger fatigue, I finally worked up the bending tip of the sturdy rod. Our fish suddenly broke the surface beside the skiff, scaring us half to death. But thrashing for a moment there on the surface was a huge sturgeon, no salmon at all. In the half-light it was a true creature of the deep—some seven feet long. How on earth had it struck my bait so hard? Now as it flailed past, striking the stern of our boat, I could see the problem. I had accidentally snagged the monster under one of its plates near its gills. Ye gods—what a mess!

In my casual approach to the morning launch I had failed to bring heavy gloves. The hide of a sturgeon that size would tear my hands in shreds as I tried to boat it or dislodge the hook. I made a half-hearted grab for its tail. "Cut the line and give it up," L.P. expostulated.

I was feeling my café royale. "A neat idea, but I need some wire cutters to get close in." Cold water splashed up over the boat. Across my aching shoulder I could see a surging white comber moving toward us from the wake of the big log carrier, churning on downstream now and whistling monotonously.

"See if you can turn us bows on. Right now!" L.P. expertly turned and in the way of things, the sturgeon, now thrashing beneath the bows, helped turn us into the looming green wave. Out went my line once more, and less than a minute later the big old lunker was gone, along with a couple hundred feet of forty pound test line wrapped around some ancient inshore pilings.

No problem of getting hook and leader disengaged. "Think of all that caviar gone to the bottom," said L.P., who loves the stuff.

"Males don't produce eggs," I yapped. "Besides, that fish was a foot and a half over the limit. Anything over sixty-six inches has to go back in the water." The weight was something else again.

"Oh, I don't know. It would depend on the fog a bit . . . the density." L.P. was lost in Sevruga thoughts, or maybe Beluga. Such desires inspire the poacher's organs of greed.

"It really depends on how scared I am. That was one spooky fish." Columbia River caviar with chopped egg and onion is God's gift. I could sense all aspects of L.P.'s fantasy.

"Maybe so, but she had beautiful green eyes."

"He," I said, as we glided once more back to our dock. The sturdy Sea Gull motor was humming beautifully, all two and one-half horses; but I was frankly thinking back once more to my eagle on the first hole. Had that been skill or plain luck? The ninth hole had definitely been luck after all; a full circle experience, going around and coming around.

INCREDIBLE LIES

We would eat some more breakfast now. My clubs needed some attention, and in my bag were the mysterious feathers. They had been soon forgotten in the excitement of last night's *Sturm und Drang* on the ninth fairway.

As our skiff nudged the pier I was frankly relieved to tie up. It was perfectly obvious. We shouldn't have gone out on the flood tide river at all. It was full of debris, swirling snags and deadheads dislodged by yesterday's unusual deluge; and made far more dangerous by a now sucking ebbtide. Luck was with me as usual. Or was it lady luck, green-eyed and seven feet long? For such luck I would give up buckets of glistening caviar—or at least one, overflowing. L.P. said nothing, conveying several significant messages through silence, including something about my judgmental powers outdoors.

I was convinced that another favorite physical activity, chopping alder and fir logs and splitting dry cedar kindling, would strengthen those long-driving power muscles. How to re-establish spacious rhythms, long abandoned, but now at last rededicated to golf? Now a burst of warm wind blowing straight upriver from Hawaii once again tickled my memory of Brookline. And I suddenly realized in a flash from the past one of the reasons for old man Gwynne's curious uneasiness. Memory is a twenty-four-hour clearing house. It was a social problem, the introduction of anarchy through athletics, or some such analysis. Lots of change going on.

For Gwynne, Sr., even in 1945, it was just a bit difficult to accept the consternating fact that a Homeric champion, such as Ouimet clearly was, could along with an increasing number of others, emerge from the ranks "up the hawse hole," as nineteenth-century limeys said. There was a profound, now inexplicable difference for class-bound Gwynne, even though the champion was from his own course.

"Damn it, sir," the patriarch once exclaimed over a much-acclaimed Thanksgiving punch, "he began to play golf for a living! And since when were professional golfers allowed into our clubhouses . . . into a gentleman's dressing room and game rooms? What do you talk about? You can't bring them home to dinner!" He was truly puzzled, poor old crustacean. And he had a terrible swing to boot.

I thought of Sarazen and the great "Haig," Walter Travis, and other early known champions; conquering semi-pros who had burned up the private courses of the north Atlantic, only to be frozen out of the gentlemen's clubhouses. Such a paradox. Steadily increasing my cedar shake supply, I chopped merrily away while thinking of new ways to approach a solid mastery of Firclad.

For one thing, there was quite a different kind of player at Firclad, with different techniques. Apparent was a working man's vigor and physique. Perhaps more ferocity than finesse, more strength than grace. Maybe coming late to the game brought a style marked for manly vigor and unconcealed tigerishness, unlike the lithe and assured grace of "the Master" and his truly elegant band. And after all, the "caddie swing" was an earned prize, available only at the price of much hard work in one's early, formative years. And some patience and tact—once learned, never forgotten—as well. Which means also knowing when to keep your mouth shut, along with eyes and ears open. To begin with, no six-year-old swing was ever adopted by a man of fifty or sixty following his physician's advice to take up golf . . . questionable advice at best. Golf courses now are renowned for a variety of strokes and attitudes, to include the medical and pathological.

· · · ·

I was suddenly thrown back over half a century plus, remembering how we quickly squelched our boyish giggles and merciless comments as the regular players arrived at the course. They came in a ragged gaggle, all within a five- or ten-minute interval; just after 2:00 on most Thursdays, and just after noon every Saturday, rain or shine, racing up the graveled roads. Car doors were opened and shut with abandon. In the 1930s, everyone who had any employment at all worked every Saturday morning. And then, too, a job to most golf players meant managerial, professional, or that of an owner. A "position," simply stated.

There was a clear-cut caste system of income and occupation which was simply a fact in a somewhat withered economy. Friday was for the ladies, the brave few, and Sunday afternoon was "mixed play" for the docile. Thursday afternoon was illicit freedom. The social scheme was frankly a simpler fabric, in no way better.

Into the locker room the regulars would rush, forever hopeful, always the eternal optimists. Quickly changing shoes and snatching bags of clubs, the early arrivals would crowd along to the first tee, ignoring blasting wind, sleet, or drenching winter rains. One stalwart would manfully opine, "I see a bit of blue off there to the west."

"The wind will open up that cloud pack," another always offered.

"Yes, it's letting up," would come a mutter. And then a pronouncement by a senior member, "Well, let's get going if we're going to play eighteen." Off they splashed. The rain fell.

Their oilskins would flash rivulets of water. Then our shoes would squish as we picked up their ever-heavier canvas and heavy leather bags. Absolutely immense, dense divots would fly through the air. We would replace the mush in a most cunning and practiced manner. What a place to learn the secrets of human nature! Clubs would be hurled in exasperation. Cool was lost. Horrendous words, better heard in the stoker's hole, were used and halfheartedly smothered and swallowed. Patience vanished. Curses of frustration would lash after the smothered hook and fading slice.

On the approach to the long walk up to the third tee above the caddie shack, the club cook would usually be staunchly waiting each Saturday just after 1:00 with huge sandwiches of freshly baked sourdough bread and slabs of spicy hot pork smothered in mustard. No cholesterol. This twenty-five cent feast was washed down with spring water so hard it rattled all the way to the bottom. And sometimes, to my childish shock, some of the men, especially those who had "gone overseas to France," would pull out a small flask for a gulp or two of moonshine bourbon or brandy. That was to get them up the hill in those days of shanks' mare golf.

Playing golf meant walking, or loping as my brothers did. Who then would have dreamed of electric carts, starting times, and fairways and greens groomed like Axminster carpets? Let's not discuss the hundred-dollar green fees for nine or eighteen. Frankly, I preferred the Mortlake tapestries of former times, shaggier, more deeply textured, more fathomless in their bold surprises. . . . Real golf is not meant for level playing fields. I chopped on in a reverie, strangely reenergized, treading the hills of memory.

. . . .

But now around my growing wood pile, baffling fogs eddied up from the river and the creek and sloughs surrounding our shingled cottage. Maybe I should best take my early "elevenses" with L.P., and should I perhaps then catch the local crowd as they arrived for their afternoon tournament with their upriver opponents? There could be but one answer. Thrust home!

In our cozy house my partner kindly left her lofty reflections about some rich and textured scholarship to suggest a true restorative, one of the

nobler cognacs. Years past we had acquired this imperative sense of interlude while working through great historical archives in Europe, be they
dank or dry. Almost like the famous Dr. Pepper slogan in carbonated
America . . . regularly at 10:00, 2:00, and 4:00 PM and (especially in the
British archives) did we infuse ourselves; always followed around 5:00 by
obscenely strong China tea and milk. Oh yes! In Russia we seemed to drink
more Crimean cognac than tea. At least I did.

My partner then remarked, "I see you have 'a thing' on your mind. I sense
your return to Firclad . . . like within minutes. But I have a roast in the oven,"
said my champion reflectively. "What do you say I slice some of this new bread
I'm working on and you carve yourself a couple of slices of roast pork with several of your favorite no-fat mustards. You can munch on the way. Am I a mind
reader? Also, this morning I won't watch while you butter your bread."

God in Heaven! How could she have known so precisely? I needed a
butter build-up for my Tin Man joints.

"Also, by the way, did you think to turn in your scorecard? A legal
one? After all, did you actually ask about the membership application?
And you could be blackballed, you know," an eyebrow raised speculative-
ly. I failed to bite.

Such a feast it was, a gorge like the days of old, and all in ten minutes.
Beautifully roasted pork is to be treasured, especially with mustard and
gobs of pepper. Butter and horseradish, too. The thought of turning in my
scorecard seemed gross. Also misleading.

I drove upriver across the dense green wetland, marveling at the ranges
of mint green tree buds which seemed to have popped out overnight.
Closely following the 55 m.p.h. road rule, I was soon working the uphill
side road like a happy field mouse through the approach maze to Firclad.
Subconsciously I then realized I had planned my supposedly impetuous

decision so that my arrival would coincide with the just-after-noon arrival of the Saturday players as in those days of the Great Depression. They came back to mind curiously, with such clarity; their clothes, shoes, wrinkles, freckled hands, gnarled fingers, and tufted ears.

· · • • •

In a reverie, their ancient, now-classic cars flashed through my mind, winding one by one up the long, graveled, dusty serpentine to "The Country Club." A Reo; an ancient Moon; two DeSotos—one of them a Brewster green four-door; then a spanking new Cord; and, in 1939, a low-slung black Continental Cabriolet roadster with red leather seats; a Chrysler Airflow driven by the hard-pounding senior circuit judge; several Ford V-8s with wire wheels; and two Plymouth coupes, one with a red rag top; and then a LaSalle. A big Buick road car vied for my attention with a DeSoto, but always the favorite was a blue and white Packard four-door convertible with the new white sidewalls. To die and go to heaven! And then of course, there was Beldon's very acceptable Chrysler coupe with a very high tan shine. And one old Stutz Bearcat, and a massive Dodge, plus my father's neat, dependable four-cylinder pickup . . . fifty years ahead of the pack. I think it was World War I surplus. But again times had changed.

• • • •

The Firclad lot was jammed! Parking our car on the side track, I walked up through the arching alders into an arena crowded not only with cars as sleek as a half-century earlier, but also a very substantial showing of pickups—more than a third. Looming above the low-slung modern cars was a large percentage of SUVs and RVs, recreational vehicles of every description. And of course, the most dramatic change, perhaps the greatest percentage of machines consisted of Japanese, or at least Asian makes. These were followed by a generous showing of Swedish, Italian, French, English, and German cars. Well, let's say a sprinkling. Times really suffer change. And there were many more cars. So much for Saturday morning toil and the fifty-hour week.

And now the so-called managerial class or factory and store owners were sporting oversized Mercedes and BMWs, two T-Birds, one new Jaguar, an ancient Bentley, and a Fairlane—plus a vintage Rolls. Toyotas stood in ranks. And of a Brewster green finish, there was none to be seen. So much for progress. Car telephones and other "fully equipped" signs abounded. And the hubbub I heard coming up from the clubhouse and the first four holes below was the cumulative roar of a fleet of powered golf carts, excrescenses not even dreamed of in the late 1930s. I then noticed a huge shed designed solely for their storage from the winter rains. There were eighty spaces! A $180,000 inventory, plus rentals.

Fortunately, the weather promised a beautiful day; also, I had already witnessed a basic fact of life: weekend golf at Firclad was not for me, certainly not in my private person mode. I was now determined—come what may—to hold it ever more close and dear. One obviously had to *wait* to play on weekends and most definitely reserve a starting time! The very thought of it! Excruciating . . . teeing off in front of fifty idling witnesses. No sir. Not my game at all!

Foremost in my thoughts and my sense of pleasure was the fact that taken though I was with Mac and the great world of golf, I "owed absolutely nothing to nobody," especially a wrinkled left-handed guru and his grassless greens. Yes, I would become a member, but not an all-around social member. Never on Saturday! Never, ever, on Sunday. I can always chop wood or, speaking of small populations, fish for salmon. Or sturgeon, steelhead trout—bullheads, even.

Tan was nearby, raking up masses of needles and twigs from yesterday's storm. Impossible to look more weather-beaten, the clubhouse still looked strangely at ease with itself, calmly accepting the loss of several courses of hand-split shingles. The all-around look was of a broad visual damage, easily remedied; and while there were ranks of blown-down trees along the fairways, there were no big holes on the horizon line or the landscape.

"It was just a bit of overdue grooming," said Tan. "In two weeks there will be no sign of yesterday's blast. Mother's in charge as usual."

He turned back to his energetic raking, but then suddenly exclaimed, "Speaking of blasts, you should hear Dad talking about your game yesterday."

"Oh no!" My privacy dream shattered.

"Oh yes. He has already turned it into an epic. You may as well be forewarned." Tan grinned wickedly, actually it bordered on a smirk. Tancred had easily penetrated my "lonely prince" pose.

I carried my bag toward the clubhouse, moving carefully along the worn-thin boardwalk bridge to the combination pro shop-restaurant. Fast-food counter better describes what I saw; a cafe crowded with attentive men of every age and description, all drinking beer, eating dogs, nachos, and burgers, and all gazing raptly at their leader, guide, and counselor, one Tarquin McMurdo. And as he turned toward the door he had the unmitigated gall to say, "And here he is, the star of the show, the new club champion, at least for today, Mr. . . . , say, what is your name, anyway? In all the excitement yesterday, I clean forgot to write down your name."

"Well, actually I didn't give it, but on the course I'd like to be called Vip; my name is V.P.P. Browne." I met his level blue-eyed gaze with one equally level. I could see that "Vip" amused him, maybe about as much as "RIP," but he was not about to believe it, not for a moment.

"Well, anyway, here's to our newest member," said Mac more gamely. "At least I hope that you are!"

"I certainly am, and to celebrate this new chapter in my life I hope you'll allow me to buy for the house." An instant roar of approval shook the room. The easy way to men's hearts.

"Well, *I* never have, so be our host," said the guru. "That's about sixty-two bottles of Henry's or Full Sail, barring two or three soda waters." But there were no dissenters in the teeming crowd, just a call for Rogue.

"But I really came in to restock my supply of golf balls." I eyed the crocks of used balls. Tan's special reserve.

Mac had a bluff response. "Well, with all the stumps and salal and high grass around here, we all agree it takes a lot of balls to play golf."

There was raucous agreement all around, but I winced once more at the sudden recollection of long ago and far away. Phrases that vibrate in the memory.

"And don't forget," Mac intoned, "so far as the high grass is concerned, I said it first. The fairways are in great shape."

"Oh, I'm sure it grew overnight, as usual," said one archly. An obviously well-worn remark. Amidst the raillery, the club clock struck noon and the players continued to sortie on to the first tee. What a cheery atmosphere it was, full of optimism, blandishment, and packs of exuberant lies. But then that was an extra dimension of the great game; an innocent merriment, sometimes. Maybe I would play occasionally on weekends. We would see. . . .

Such verve! And I knew without reflection there would be such an astonishing variety of swings and inventive ways in which to "address the ball." I had quickly come to that notion the preceding day on the third and eighth fairways, where I had happened upon two cans of snoose, one an unopened tin of Copenhagen nestled in the rough. In my mind's eye, loggers of immense power swung clubs like matchsticks, so used were they to felling trees with broad axes—or so my reverie cast it. And they had started to play late in life. Power to the people! Style is not all. A sharp eye on the ball comes first. Chain saws didn't enter my mind. At least not for reverie.

The truth is I knew that countless men and women were now taking great pleasure in golf, a game somehow less available to them in leaner years and before television unveiled the quirky game's intense and instant pleasures. And so many players! The heady enthusiasm was infectious. There was more energy—much more whooping and hollering, much less austere and centripetal. The sun sprang up in the bright blue heaven, full blaze; and my God, out on the fairway, one bull-of-the-woods even now actually began to peel off his sweatshirt. Yes! Bare! At 165 yards, I could see he had a huge red and green dragon running up around his upper right arm and across his shoulder in an unbelievable design, pointing vaguely down south. Tattooed to the max. Fantastic, not to say stunning.

"Well, why not?" I thought. But my dad would have pitched over face first into the creeping bent, had there been any. No shirt! A terrible gaffe. On the golf fairways with no shirt when ties were recommended. On the other hand, this was not the 1920s, 1930s, or 1950s; this was the last decade of the twentieth century, a very different proposition. So on with the tournament and the sheer fun of it.

The clubhouse continued to buzz with bonhomie and prospects of a beautiful, maybe windless day. And then, too, not everyone started his day out casually ordering sixty-two bottles of beer. Life's little pleasures!

Somewhat agog, but game, Mrs. Mac was still pulling them from the cooler with several eager helpers. I like an occasional gesture, the big ones most of all.

We stepped out on Mac's battered porch overlooking the first tee. Oh yes, the course was plenty crowded and there was an intent line-up dutifully waiting on Mac's starting times. Yes, pros were certainly kings these days; and especially ones who owned the course to boot. What a study of upward mobility! And pros were the lords of their special creations. The postwar years were different, and again the players here were physically just a bit different as well. Slightly longer arms, I thought, and more strength through the chest and across the shoulders; certainly not the same as most "gym physiques" in town. And a more explosive power was delivered to the ball in sundry, sometimes riveting ways. Determined, yes; graceful . . . well, seldom.

. . . .

My mind roved back to the men and women of the thirties; a different breed. They seemed wirier, maybe a little smaller; more compact. I realized that several men whom I had assessed back then as chronic coughers had, in fact, been gassed in the trench wars during World War I. They had been slower players, more deliberate and usually more accurate, but their endurance was less. And balls cost money. They were apt to be more reflective, although not morose; introspective covered it nicely, along with determination. They swore silently, except for an occasional volcanic outburst of hair-raising gaminess.

One memorable man back then, slight, grizzled, quiet except for his cough and with a tawny port complexion, was a splendidly dependable putter. Red Blackman had twice beaten my younger brother for the club championship in the mid-thirties. Phlegm was his.

The betting that last day was against him, not to mention his age, but defying all odds and reason he finished the last nine holes with but seven nerveless putts. Red had sunk a long approach shot in a crosswind on the rolling sixteenth and to finish, chipped in from the apron on the eighteenth. He also finished my young brother, who gamely said that he'd been taught "an unexpected lesson." Red's lion-like eyes glowed with deep pleasure. He often remarked later that my brother was a sportsman, even at fifteen, but that it might be best to learn early how to lose once or twice.

· · · ·

But now here was Mac again, very much front and center. After all, this was his domain.

"Glad you're back so soon. Are you really going to sign up today?"

"Well, I hope so."

"So do I, Vip, because that will make us exactly two hundred members—that is, if your missus signs on too."

"Well, I hadn't thought along that line just yet, Mac."

"We need you both. Doc Niblett, our dentist, died on us last month and one of the pulp supervisors across the river was transferred to a mill down south. We don't miss *him* much, but his wife was one of our best players, man or woman." I thought of the Hoyt sisters . . . .

"Gee . . . well, let's start by saying, how much? What are your greens fees?"

"Eight dollars for eighteen holes, or all you want to play for ten."

"Is that senior-citizen?"

"Oh, oh . . . $6.50 for eighteen, and all you can handle beyond that for another dollar. A total of $7.50."

"How about a life membership?" was my canny response.

"I've never heard of such a thing! What would you think when I sold my course to some Oriental industrialist? You would lose out."

"I'd think you would live to a ripe old age. And the owner still."

"I've already done that. Any other ideas while I'm looking over the used balls? Some are livelier than others."

"Well, how much for a year?" Again a pause.

"For one?"

"Well yes, at least for now."

"Well, let's say $150 a year."

I fell silent, much as I love banter. In fact I was speechless. How could this be? If I played every day that would be . . . no, it didn't seem possible. The figures weren't coming up.

"And . . . for cash I'll throw in a dozen good, used golf balls. . . ."He bounced a lively one off the floor boards for effect.

I waited silently, following my dad's teachings of long ago. Don't rush, look reflective. Close the deal, but with a stately pace.

"And a new glove, too; yours looks just a bit rotten . . . well, worn, anyway."

I paused, disbelieving, reassuming my thousand-yard stare.

"And six free lessons . . . for the missus."

"I blinked and stared west.

"Ninety minutes each."

"L.P., my wife, is just beginning."

"She can have all the lessons she wants . . . my undivided attention, when I'm not mowing and changing the cups. Never on Sundays."

AN INTERLUDE

Pause. Stateliness.

"At $125 . . . providing the missus is a senior citizen."

"She will be, in time. And L.P. will love to learn the great game from you rather than from me. I value our special friendship."

"Then it's a done deal?"

"Absolutely right. Just give me a pen and add two new members to the roster."

"Great! . . . then let me get this tournament moving along faster. Most of these guys have already played their first nine. Then you and I can play. Okay? Maybe the holes we left out yesterday."

Mac cocked a look up at me. I heartily agreed with his plan.

No one had yet crashed a drive off the first tee as far as mine the day before. At least not yet. I looked high above for *my* eagle. The immense aquamarine sky was empty of everything but promise. The balls continued to crack off toward greens, and an occasional expletive rich beyond expectations or memory wafted up to my perch. Much better than cricket bats.

My family would love this unassuming but guileful course. Perhaps this would be the place to bring my oldest brother back into play, he who carried an unusual personal record of four double eagles, recorded on three different golf courses. Take that, Guinness! Not to mention a clutch of aces.

This might stimulate some renewed interest and vigor for him. And why not think big, as I had so vaingloriously done that long-ago afternoon at Yale? Yes, he would instantly be at one with the course, and truly the first and seventh holes were made for double eagles. Perhaps none had yet been recorded. And they were crafted for his powerful stylized drive, one just skirting the desperate dangers inherent in a smothered hook. I knew all too well.

My beer was long gone and the crowd had thinned away in their foursomes. They moved steadily toward the greens through golden sunshine.

INCREDIBLE LIES

THE FOURTEENTH HOLE

Mac suddenly appeared at my shoulder with his own Henry's. "What do you say we have our game now?" he queried. He really was tireless. There he capered, merry and bright and never giving way. Maybe the doctors had it wrong; it was far better to be a greenskeeper than a golfer. Again he examined my much-reduced bag with little approval. Firclad did not demand twenty, or even the legal fourteen. And gifts can become burdens without some practical winnowing.

The flock was strung out well ahead of us, and Mrs. Mac was busily organizing her record-keeping accounts to enter the tallies as the first competitors came off the "eighteenth." In a surprise move, Mac turned us and walked up toward the fifth fairway. He motioned toward a heavily planked stairway leading to the left directly above us.

"We go up here, on to this elevated tee. I call it the fourteenth."

"Oh, I see. No place for a golf cart addict."

"No, but follow me up here," he said with his typical spryness.

I was feeling a stiffness you couldn't purchase from the exercise of several hundred long-disused muscles in yesterday's wind and rain. No one had prepared me for the stiffness of the long sixties . . . but then, there was Mac! Several years older, at least!

"This is what turns the fifth hole into the fourteenth," said Mac, savoring his landscaping ingenuity. "You have a completely different sense of the approach to the green." How clever.

And of course he was right. What I had somehow missed yesterday was an almost Palladian effect, bordering on ordered Herculean. Immense, vertical, pillared fir trees marched along the upper side of the sloping fairway, playing off toward the south in a splendid colonnade grander than all of Bernini's dreams for St. Peter's Roman triumph. Firclad indeed! And high above the serried trunks, a densely green, rich, and ragged canopy of needled foliage. I noted with alarm the trunks here and there were splotched with red paint.

"Mac, are those magnificent trees marked for falling?" I exclaimed.

"Oh no! Not to worry. Those are just my out-of-bounds signs. And the rhododendrons there mark the 100- and 200-yard markers."

The rhodies were just coming into blossom. *Giganticas*! From our dramatically elevated site I could also spy a big bird wheeling on the far-off horizon. He was careening and stooping, warding off a swarm of raucous crows. Bad cess to them. My eagle was on patrol.

"Increase and multiply" was surely the apt phrase for Firclad country. No wonder David Douglas had rhapsodized so long ago over the bounteous trees in his quirky Scottish way. It was a landscape for the gods, with just enough bite to keep one lithe and lean. In stark contrast I recalled a session in the mid-forties, my first game in a semi-tropical atmosphere. Humidity and golf are still mutually exclusive as far as I'm concerned, even though I am older and stiffer in joints I didn't even know about back then. The course of memory was Seminole, near Palm Beach; and until the excitement years later in the alligator swamp at Puerto Vallarta, it was my best tropical memory of big time golf.

....

What I still remember most vividly was the lush, tough Bermuda grass all over the ocean strand of Palm Beach and the mass of wild flamingoes which had invaded the course during the rusticating days of World War II.

My host swore when he saw the birds. They were bold and had come to believe the somewhat neglected course was their own feeding ground. For some reason the birds were attracted to the endless acres of white sand contained in the countless bunkers. Not me. I was enchanted by the long rolling greens, the misty sheen of the late-December sun playing off the serpentine spray swirling in from the surf bordering the last few holes. This was before "Prince" Hogan hove into view to place his monarchical stamp on this seaside links; and how right Little Ben was. Seminole is a most "fair and meritorious course." It was timeless.

I was carried away with the whole South Atlantic scene that day, but my game seemed off. Even in one's early twenties an occasional hangover dropping from a great height can mar the day. So it was with me. After lunch in the magnificently appointed men's grill we lazily started the second nine, and in the way of youth, life was suddenly restored; perhaps through the infusion of a quart of fresh-squeezed orange juice from a new brand named Indian Creek, located just nearby.

Whatever it was, the second round started off with a bang, with four of us playing evenly. Four is at least one and frankly two more players than I really like to have along on my idiosyncratic games. But we were off with my unconventional birdie on the tenth, where fervent thanks were privately offered up for the slight spin on my ball and the ocean wind which guided me over the gaping right-hand traps guarding the green. The very straightforward eleventh I bogeyed. I was lucky to blast out of the three-quarter-length trap complex. The next two holes were played in a humid trance as the wind died down and a very hot, increasingly foreign sun bored down on the fairways.

Hogan later stated "the best par four anywhere in the world" was the sixth at Seminole. But one of the best par threes is the beautiful thirteenth, an emerald resting in a desert of sand. If the pin had been in securely I would have had my first ace . . . maybe. My ball bounced once and hit the pin a hard rattle a foot below the flag and dropped down three inches from glory. On the other hand, maybe I was lucky playing into the stout onshore wind. My partners took a four, a five, and a six. If the pin had been vertical I might have missed it—and the whole green. I remember, too, it was my first game with sunglasses.

On the long fourteenth I ran up a double bogie over the more than 300 yards. Variable gusts were thwarting my game plan. I was buckling. But it seemed as though my host was interested only in reaching the fifteenth and sixteenth holes. When I scrambled out of the tangled mess of the four-teenth I was, despite the mayhem, even then one over par, frankly not bad for anyone on a new course.

As we approached the fifteenth tee all I could see ahead was a mass of palmettos rattling away on the port side. My very silent and attentive cad-die observed in a mighty outburst, "Well, suh, here it is." But there was lit-tle I could make out on the low-lying course besides the ocean's horizon. Perhaps it was just as well. My caddie handed me what I had come to regard as an extra long driver. Our foursome fell silent, and I thought my host must be reflecting on one of his mammoth real estate ventures. Between General Eisenhower's armistice and the catastrophe of Castro's arrival, he managed eventually to acquire around one-eighth of lower Florida, excluding the Everglades; but he had not acquired me as a son-in-law. But now, his silence registered a simple trepidation about golfing life beyond our immediate horizon line. So I simply hunched down and hit my Titleist as hard as I could and it went as far as it could go, straight and true. Which was a long distance in those days.

If someone had better described the hole to me I might have played short and hit the water hazard or splashed as I sidled a stroke around to the left. And furthermore, there were two broad sheets of water to avoid, both blind. I did; and then without thinking twice, I hit a three iron, snugged up to the hole, and missed a short putt for a sparkling eagle. My host purred. An eagle would have been, by southern standards, well, almost too much good luck, not quite gentlemanly; whereas a birdie looked brilliant. It's rather hard to explain, but at the time it seemed fact.

On the sixteenth I simply repeated the shots on a slightly shorter fairway over sand, but the sea wind rattling in the palm fronds was a horrendous distraction. Nonetheless, I got another birdie. On the seventeenth I shot first and again almost holed out in a layout very much like the emerald thirteenth. I would call those greens almost matched stones . . . Brazilian. Exhilarating. By now our foursome was carrying immense tension and it seemed some news of our exploits had carried ahead to the Seminole clubhouse, even though I was then just three under par as I recall it now. Maybe two . . . or four.

The eighteenth snugs the ocean shore as does the seventeenth, the fourteenth tee, and the thirteenth green. But as I idly tossed up a bit of mist-softened grass into the air, the late afternoon was producing something for the Beaufort scale. Big time. And the eighteenth, as nearly as I could determine from the card, was almost one hundred yards shorter than the fifteenth, but a cranky dogleg.

THE FOURTEENTH HOLE

For some reason I impetuously rejected the three iron my caddie carefully handed me and exulted over my tactical position. I stepped up and struck the ball with everything I had. Everyone else appeared to be in trouble here and there. My ball was not in sight as we strolled toward the finish. When we reached the true fairway I could see an ever-increasing crowd and late luncheon types sauntering toward the back swell of the eighteenth, taking their ease in the soft grass beneath the Cole Porter palms. Oh no, a gallery! My uneasy sense of privacy vanished in a trice. Faster than you-know-what. At that point I realized that my drive in a following wind had rolled across the green, continuing along to the upper sand trap.

Whatever caused me to so misjudge the onshore wind I'll never know. Happily for the increasing gallery, my partners all made grand recovery shots, grouped two on the green and one just on the apron, but all below the cup. My sand blast shot kissed the lip of the left-hand sand trap and rolled down and across, just beneath the heavy salt-crusted grass edging the lower trap. In my panic to get out of the sand I simply lost my head, and raised it. Slow and easy? No. Fast and frantically? Yes! I then clenched the newly designed wedge and blasted my ball again into an even deeper trap on the far side of the green. My partners looked blank. My once-proud caddie sent a long look of agony across the ocean water down toward Cuba. Three strokes and still entrapped. It was a nightmare.

Maybe some of the older Seminoleans still remember the young tiger who came to the eighteenth three under his first time at Seminole and slunk at last into the clubhouse four over. But just as the Prince said, it truly is "a fair course." Unbeknownst, until years later, I had more than anticipated Sam Snead's great debacle under somewhat similar circumstances on the same course.

That night I brooded on Mussolini's bitter reflection on the basic weakness of Italian colonial acquisitions. Big appetites, but very poor teeth. My golf game suffered the same stress. It made no difference that the magnificent Snead would suffer the same; but that's what an erstwhile correspondent later reported to me. And all that was long ago.

· · · ·

I slowly returned north from my golfing reverie in southern climes 3,000 miles distant to face the business at hand: the realities of Firclad and my southpaw Nestor. How Mac loved his course; and why not? Carved out of nothing it was, and by his own hands and mowers.

The foursome leaving the green ahead of us held some interest. Of course I was a mature man now; let's say more than mature—perhaps overripe. Notwithstanding, my perspective had changed sharply; these men of Firclad generally seemed more than a bit bigger and stronger, even than those I had observed with child's eyes. They were also more exuberant, as witness the occasional whoops and jibes as good shots were made and long putts unexpectedly sunk, and short putts missed. They were certainly less chained to etiquette and proper form. There was something to be said here on both sides. Enthusiasm holds much natural charm.

There was a whoop as I fired a long hook, green high but very likely out-of-bounds in the fir colonnades flank marching up the sloping fairway. I burrowed for another ball, but Mac said to wait. He had a feeling my ball might be playable. Go with the experts is my motto. He then lofted a left-handed spellbinder just over the flag to the back slope and the foursome ahead applauded as his shot lazed its way back downhill and cozied in next to the flag. He bowed and expressed some stage wonderment. I had some feeling he had made that same snuggle shot a hundred times.

He was right about my drive. As we strolled up through the acres of low-lying field daisies I could see my ball perched almost next to an out-of-bounds stake. No problem, there were inches to spare. At least three, anyway. Again I observed the Palladian colonnade. A northern paradise. The trees were in a class of their own.

With some more undeserved luck I dropped my pitch shot in close to Mac's lie, and I gratefully scored a par—putting out as he did. The continuation of our game with a par on the fifth, that is to say the elevated fourteenth, was frankly reassuring. I had expected the worst. Now I almost sensed the vaunted "feel" returning, even though the wind was sharp as we waited on the exposed tee.

THE FIFTEENTH HOLE

Far ahead, near the middle of the "fifteenth" fairway, a superb piece of young brawn was addressing his ball. His power practice swing was easy, effortless. Thirty-five is a perfect age.

"He's their great white hope," said Mac. "You can see he started younger than most. All the effortless rhythm is there. More than our team has, anyway."

"He looks programmed like some machine-tooled product," I ventured. Was there something familiar in all of that precision?

"I know. It's almost too good. Some of the excitement leaves with the arrival of predictability. It's certainly more Prestwick than St. Andrews." Yes, Mac would always surprise me.

"Maybe that's good, but it's also apt to be boring. And it sure plays hell with the competition. He looks just a little skittish."

Mac gave a knowing left-handed whack off, slightly to the right. A perfect position. With all the force of a giant magnet my ball was drawn toward a large metal water tower screened by a clump of trees, directly in the center of the "fifteenth" fairway about 250 yards away. My ball struck hard with a resonating boom high up on the tower wall. A more-than-public shot echoing across the fairways.

"It sounds almost armorial, medieval, and arcane," I muttered. "A sound from the dim past." My fancy was taken with the idea of a roving knight striking some shield hung beside the tower. Somewhat far-fetched, I suspected. Would some kind of foul dragon emerge from the copse, crawling as it were, deep from the slime of some fetid Virginia swamp? Reptilian and quite out of place.

Then on the wind along came some derisive hoots from the far-off green, including "Brawn." Really, too much exuberance.

"And aside from all that you're out of bounds," Mac primly reported. "There's no doubt about it."

"I don't believe that. How can there be an out-of-bounds area in the middle of the fairway?"

"I suppose it's strange," he conceded, "but think of it as a vertical lake rather than a tower of water." What would he think of next? Out of bounds, my eye. The tower was an unnatural hazard, for openers.

I was slightly disgusted, but as I turned to pick up my clubs a strange and wonderful sight caught my eye. Emerging from the copse around the great stump came a slow-moving elk herd of varying sizes, led once again by Lucky Pierre's, now dragging some trailing ivy vines from his velvety antlers. There were now five mothers moseying along with him—and yes, by Jove, seven calves! Two of the lady elks had thrown twins, and they had to be the children of Lucky Pierre's; his own special club. Perhaps the only one in a twenty-mile radius. Lucky continued his casual saunter—a natural leader—missing limb or no. On the links perhaps "missing member" would be the more apropos word.

There was a murmur and then some congratulatory shouting and applause along the fairways. After all, how many courses boasted a resident herd of elk? And how many irate greens committees would want to, I rejoined to myself. Mac was looking north without comment, but I was certain he sensed some new life in the wild distraction playing out behind him. The calves continued to wobble across toward the stile where I had first seen the expectant mothers just twenty-four hours earlier. Such a landscape it was; everything seemed to grow before one's eyes, including the herds. Mac's mind was elsewhere.

And then once more I reviewed something of my hazy tour of southern fairways. Was it just yesterday, last century, or another life? Our country is varied and vast. Time and space elude controls.

By way of explanation for my long lapse I queried Mac about Seminole. Did he know it?

"Oh sure. That's where all the millionaires and flamingoes play around."

"From what I've heard lately there seem to be even more millionaires and fewer birds down there. But frankly, Mac, I prefer the seagulls you feature at Firclad." Far off I could see Lucky's herd just sidling into the tall ferns and huckleberries off so-called number seven. Lucky "Lucky Pierre's" . . . may thy herds increase.

My ball was sitting just off to the side and not out of bounds by a short foot. Ha ha! There was a thin chance to roll it through a narrow opening in the alder grove to the apron beyond. Without thought I seized it. By George, it worked. Concentrate. Focus!

Mac made no comment as we both holed-out with pars. He was in something of a study, and an easy silence walked with us to the next tee.

"Do you and the missus have any kids, Vip?"

"Oh yes. We have four children. At least I think we had them. It all seemed to happen so fast; we can't believe they've grown up and flown. I keep recounting. Did they really come and then go?"

THE FIFTHTEENTH HOLE

"Do they live in town?"

"No, it's funny really, this wind reminded me somehow of our daughter who lives in London, that is, down the Thames in greater London. Their ancient and revered house is right on the edge of Blackheath."

"Don't say it, Vip! They play right in the cradle room of golf? You know what Blackheath has always meant to golf!"

"Well, not quite, Mac. Golf is expressly forbidden on the Heath today, but on some moonlit evenings the neighbors sneak in a few iron shots! Happily it's still a big open piece of parkland even now. I've had a few hunter's moon shots myself, just for soul food. In the footsteps of the Stuarts describes it best, especially Charles I and II."

"I can just remember seeing the edge of the Heath during the war. My special unit was steaming the Thames downstream toward the open sea and France. One of the Limeys pointed out Newton's meridian tower up above the river mist at Greenwich. That was my anchor. For some reason I knew that Blackheath was a six or seven iron shot beyond." He was looking a long way back, something in the manner of my own musings.

"I know some of the British courses, but only one in mainland Europe," I offered. "Hardly a course, though."

The wind continued to ruffle the rose-limbed alders on the northern slope behind us. It was a splendid rise of roseate color that maybe some took for granted. I thought, oh to be a Girtin or a Turner out "'scaping" on a day like this. The range of soft colors did genuinely defy description, even for master watercolorists. Cotman would have got it just right, no doubt in my mind. Especially since the undulatory hills rose and fell like his seas.

The Hanovers suddenly came to mind. Golf was not for the Electors. Would things be very different if the Stuarts had endured? There was no doubt in my mind that there would be more open spaces for golf than horses, and an improved cuisine . . . but then what? One couldn't buy the unfailing taste of "Prinny," more augustly known as George the Fourth.

THE SIXTEENTH HOLE

My first look down the "sixteenth" fairway produced no memories, but the following wind stimulated other thoughts. The Master had frankly deplored wind. He considered the worst games in his special book those played on British courses, especially English links near the Channel. Those quirky, spurting gusts of wind off the saltwater wreaked havoc with scorecards; and certainly it was no better on the French side, whatever they suggested.

A sudden inspiration struck me then, one which I would later turn over and weigh more than once. Serendipity again.

"Mac, I've only played one French course, and it's not any links to remark on . . . that is, except for some unusual historical associations."

"Well, I've only played one myself—but it's a game I'll never forget. In fact, it wakes me up sometimes."

"The game or the score?"

"I mean the place— June, 1944, just off Utah Beach."

"Mac, are you and I both thinking of a little nine-hole Normandy course just back from the dunes? It has to be, there's only one course along Utah Beach. A links, I mean."

"Well, maybe there's more than one now. After all, it's over forty years ago. The fact is, being around you I started thinking kind of backwards, along historical lines. When I mentioned Greenwich earlier I started then counting back to when I saw Blackheath."

"Counting the years, you mean?"

"Actually, for that time I can count each day and lots of the hours. There was just nothing like those few weeks, not ever to be repeated either. Thank God!"

"So, did you come up with some special date?"

"Well, I came up with an anniversary. Exactly fifty years less three weeks ago, I saw Blackheath on the way down the Thames, sailing around Dover to join the invasion fleet at Portsmouth."

"Don't say fifty years, because that's half a century. It still seems like yesterday to me. Let's save it all up for the seventy-fifth—which is practically tomorrow." Mac nodded at that.

It was extraordinary, but we were on target with the exact same tiny seaside course. Once again, I had spotted the flags above the dunes thirty years ago. L.P. was driving us along the low beach road on our first trip to the Allied invasion sites. I was reading the ordnance map. A tiny sprawl of a course snuggled amongst some ancient vacation cottages strung along the empty but forever famous beach. There had to be a story here from Mac, so I urged.

"Well, there's not much to tell. Like several thousand others, I had gone in to the beach on D-Day, but not 'til the afternoon. There was junk all over the sand and surf. We were running up a long wire mat past quite a crowd of our guys already dug in next to the marsh. The next thing I knew we were piling right into a deep sand bunker. It seemed so familiar, like a training exercise except all of a sudden I saw the little red flag just ahead hanging at an angle. I knew right away where I was. We might just be home free."

THE SIXTEENTH HOLE

"You would never know the place today. Every trap is raked. But I suppose there were more traps after D-Day."

"Boy, you chose the right word. We were still raked by heavy fire from the hillsides beyond the marshes. It was deadly. The Germans had years of time to tape their fields of fire, and those artillery spotters were walking up the fairways and chewing up the greens with their 88's and mortars."

"Ye gods, this is a real golfing story! What did you do then?"

"Well, that's when we started really digging, and that's when I got my first and last European golf game organized."

Mac was savoring the recollection now. So much so that he ignored the wind as he stepped up to the tee. McMurdo then calmly rifled two drives deep into the woods. A long, very deep hook. Hoots were heard in the distance. Firclad members had very sharp eyes.

"I'd better re-focus. This is not good for my image," Mac confided, drawing balls from his bag. "But anyway, we were digging like sand hogs under the lip of the bunker, and guess what?"

"Okay, okay. What?"

"I was piling the sand up like crazy and I suddenly turned up a nest of golf balls . . . two dozen or so."

"You mean they were stashed in the trap?"

"I guess some crane or squirrel, or maybe some weirdo gull had been gathering them up like eggs. The rest of that day and night and all of the next day I memorized the names of French and English golf balls while the Germans slowly moved their heavy stuff along the road system across the tidal swamp between us. But they never ever really left us alone. I guess they could give up some French landscape, all right, but they didn't want to lose all that Normandy butter and eggs and the only golf course south of Deauville."

"Not to mention the Calvados, I bet. So what happened?"

"A couple of days later things lightened up a bit, and at dawn I went over to the shell of a house where a big Tiger tank had been hiding inside the walls. He had cut out on June sixth and blew up on the seventh. I knew I was on the right track, because it was actually the greenskeeper's shack. Part of it, anyway."

"And?"

"Well, you know we say it takes a lot of balls to play golf, but you have to have some clubs too."

"The way your face is lighting up I have an even stronger feeling why you remember your first Continental game. Give me the skinny, as we used to say then." Mac was deep in the story now.

"Well, I think maybe that German battalion commander was a golfer, because there was a make-do set of clubs pieced together in an old leather map case. During the next few days things calmed down and I managed to play the full nine holes a couple of times."

"But Mac, I don't get it! You don't mean you found a set of left-handed clubs?" He really had me going now.

"Oh no! That was too much to ask. . . . You see, I just turned myself around and played backwards." He more than guffawed, hard and long.

There was no getting around it. I'd been had. But then I drove my ball straight down the fairway with a slight hook which added at least another fifteen yards. A good 320 yards.

"You won't believe it, but Ike came along touring with the King and Omar and Monty. The King and Ike loved golf, and they spotted me and waved. Churchill even flashed the V sign, but Monty just looked down that pointy nose." Games! What a moment in history. They should have stopped. "Always smell the flowers," advised Walter Hagen.

THE SIXTEENTH HOLE

"I'll put down near yours," said Mac, still savoring his neat joke on me. "There's no point in going down in those woods; it's more like a tropical rain forest. Tan can look those balls up some day. "We both lofted a six iron close in to the pin, thinking faraway thoughts. People now think D-Day was a pushover, along with a lot of other things taken for granted.

. . . .

Yes, I was definitely on the same track with Mac, on the same beach and golf course two long screaming drives from the old French sea fortress of St. Vaast-la-Hougue. L.P. and I never tire of examining the Normandy scene whatever the seasons or century we choose. I would return to those special haunts any time. Napoleon said "Spain is not Europe," and Normandy and Brittany truly are other countries, Paris notwithstanding. I remember so well that L.P. and I had driven briskly along the hard-packed parapet road in a bright May sun. The wind off the sea was lifting a bit of sand from Utah Beach. I was intently examining some offshore markers for the massive Dutch-English sea battle in the seventeenth century called Le Hogue. I almost missed the small flags flapping in my peripheral vision. It took some minutes for my visual cortex to register the odd fact that the small golf course was lurking back behind the clutch of houses crouched in the dune swales. Hand brakes were applied and tires smoked! The Van de Veldes and other sea painters were forgotten.

When L.P. and I turned our Renault around and raced back into the little car park, the attendant at the semi-private course seemed almost puzzled by my interest and enthusiasm.

"To find a golf course on Utah Beach! Right on the beach, *sur la plage*, on the shingle, on the strand. Oh my!"

"But of course it is a beach, Monsieur. *Oui*, some call it, as you say, Utah Beach. But it is designed for invasions, *n'est-ce pas*? Roman galleys landed here, and Vikings, and then the English and Spaniards and Dutch, too. But yes, it's true we had not established our golf course then, not even the game that we know, not until later." I took note of the possessive. A better game, of course.

"Perhaps this is one of the first courses!" I exclaimed.

To see a Norman look dubious is a memorable thing. Later that eventful evening in the venerable Lion d'Or, L.P. mused over the fine Calvados. I was dreaming of the oysters and the rabbit stew. Okay, *Forestiére*. An ageless favorite. L.P. opened the conversation.

"I've been thinking about the immense beach we examined today. I suppose it may always be called Utah Beach now. And yet, I wonder. Time and space, et cetera."

"And you were wondering . . . ?"

"When we were looking at it with the manager, or whatever, I was thinking about Caesar's galleys and Viking ships. What a place to run up a few sea boats for a fast foray, food and ladies fair, together with lots of plunder. After all, that was the way of the world then."

I took a generous swig of applejack. "Good show," said I. "Mostly all of it. Should we particularize?"

"No, my idiot, I was then thinking of a much later time, and with some sense of puzzlement. Have the British mentioned, or do they, with that bottomless reach of history and anecdote, mention who else landed at this precise spot?"

She illuminated her blue, gray-green eyes and awaited my answer. None immediately forthcoming. But I ventured, "So okay. I'm not going to play the 'it wasn't so and so' game; that's too revealing. Who was this worthy standard bearer?"

"You know who it is, my darling. Fearless Edward the Third. Father to the Black Prince."

"Oh yes. Of course . . ." I dragged it on. "And did their caddies attend them?"

"I happen to remember that he landed his army at that exact site, right there at St. Vaast-la-Hougue on July 12, not quite 600 years before D-Day. There really should be a historical marker there. His bowmen could have hit Admiral Ramsey's inshore destroyers. Some of their bows were right up on the sand flats at Utah. And at Sword, too."

She paused. "I can't believe the English, especially, could forget that campaign. After all, Edward was on his way to Crécy, the first of the Big Three. And his fleet, moving along the Norman shoreline here, actually entered the Orne River at Ouistreham, just the way the Canadians and British did on June 6. Uncanny, really."

"The Big Three," I said. "I trust you refer to Crécy, Poitiers, and Agincourt."

Silent approval. L.P. reflected a moment. "And then the English bowmen used yew instead of Welsh elm. They knocked out the French crossbow men on the Orne bridges above the Caen canal just where the Oxford and Bucks Light Infantry achieved everlasting glider fame with their pre-dawn crash landings led by Major John Howard and Sergeant Wallwork."

I was gaping, although never surprised by these buckets of knowledge splashed over me. Always with the dates, names, and numbers. But this was almost too much. I remained transfixed as L.P.'s incredible outpouring continued.

INCREDIBLE LIES

"Anyway," said my unstoppable chronicler, "what I really want to chat about are the bows; not the unpolished wild elm of your tribal forebears, darling, but the English yew bows carried by Edward's archers."

But then I remonstrated. "My canny ancestors in the Marches used to stand on their land holdings with one leg in Wales and the other in England. They knew more than a bit about the Marches. And there's more that goes with that, too. Give me some credit!"

"I'm sure," said L.P. archly. "Anyway, what I want to quote now is ancient Bishop Latimer who was taught to shoot the bow as a boy. He said he was given larger bows as he increased in size, 'for all men shall never shoot well unless they be brought up on it.' What do you make of that, *mon ami*?"

"What do you mean . . . what?"

"Well, how about your hickory shafts and the great game of golf? Would it help you to get some stronger and maybe longer clubs? Or maybe some with yew or elm shafts instead of hickory . . . or just more play every day?"

I know that my mouth was open. What could I say? What would the Master say about this half-formed dream of glory? Was it valid? I still don't know. The steel shaft arrived soon after.

• • • •

But meanwhile, back at Firclad, Mac and I holed out once more and I mused at the wonder of it all. Memory, blessed memory . . . how selective it can be. I don't even remember the utterly unbelievable apple tart and heavy cream we shared.

A NECESSARY INTERLUDE

There seems to be more golf excitement in the Firclad story than I can handle. Nothing like it will ever happen to me again . . . for sure. Let me say the next two holes more than outdid themselves. It would be almost all right to say they outplayed themselves, not to mention Mac and me. Some days are forever remembered, as are one or two weekends.

But now let me jump ahead just a bit. This golf adventure can't be told just plain and simple, because I see now that there was nothing simple about it. There's nothing simple about magic. Anyway, about an hour later in an exalted frame of mind I was speeding along home from Firclad. I tried to keep the hidden highway trooper, 55 m.p.h., and Mac all in close focus. As I rolled through the low and luxuriant wetlands approach to our century-old retreat above the tidewater, two outraged herons flapped away from our frog and wapato pool. Their flying scat registered emphatic disdain. I rounded the corner onto the graveled parking safely above the lapping tide line that sometimes backed right into our car park. I cut the motor and spooked a quail covey as I slammed the door to announce my safe arrival home.

The noise failed to disturb a large but still immature eagle perched in an immense Caspar Friedrich hemlock which marked the site of an ageless

Indian campground across on the opposite, downriver side of our stream. No doubt the young bird was observing some trespasser. Me, for openers.

As I pulled my clubs and gear from the trunk, L.P. cracked open the big red door. She knew, oh yes, telepathic L.P. knew. Necromancy, I suppose. "How did it go?" she queried. "Are you a member—or on probation, as wisdom would dictate?"

"They accepted *me* without demurral. Unwisely, they also accepted you."

"Oh, fine!"

"The clubhouse seems momentarily short of cash. Mac even accepted my check without the array of backup numbers most people automatically demand today."

"So I'm a member! Does he know I have no clubs. . . no, uh, handicap, and most importantly, no . . . skills?"

"What do you say we go to a spontaneous party at the club tonight, and you can tell Mac yourself?"

"*Carpe diem* has always been my motto. And this does seem the right time to plunge on golf lessons." She waited for more.

"For one thing, he'll be your professional teacher, southpaw though he is. But let me tell you, L.P., he'll promise you anything tonight."

"So why tonight, my hero?"

"Because this afternoon on the so-called seventeenth hole Mac had his first hole in one!"

"An ace!"

"Yes, and what an ace? Like Robin, he split the arrow!"

"Tell me more, and pronto, while I mix your Negroni pitcher."

"He was flashing a brassie around, but then the wind veered toward the southwest. Mac sorted in his bag and pulled out a specially shaped persimmon spoon with a hickory shaft. Ninety years old, at least."

A NECESSARY INTERLUDE

"And . . . ?"

"But then he suddenly changed to an iron . . . a long one. He never takes a real practice swing, so the next thing I knew the ball went off with just a little slice. Then it dropped like a stone and cracked the wood flag shaft about a yard above the cup. It simply crashed down in the hole. 'Exactly 109 yards,' he said."

L.P. was properly impressed, as perfection in all things pleases her. She had already reconstructed the event in her mind, with some trimmings. "You know, L.P., I've never had an ace and I have never even been playing with anyone who had one."

"You'll have one some day; probably two or three before all the smoke clears away." She was a true believer, really L.P. to the max.

"Maybe I will join you. I'm fatally attracted by perfection."

I nodded in agreement, subconsciously including myself.

"And I would like to split the arrow, too, the way Mac did."

"So why not? Speaking of which, look at that stony-faced eagle across there sucking up our conversation. Really rude."

At that moment the grand young bird launched itself, traveling across our range at eleven o'clock and power diving down out of sight toward the shore behind our huge cedar tree. We heard the splash. Just one.

L.P. shivered slightly, sensing life and death behind the arras, but obviously an osprey and not an eagle. We would learn.

"So what's the dress code for ladies of the links?"

"Anything with tartan in it, my pet," said I, savoring my Negroni goblet. Another goblet, a warm fire, and day-long braised lamb shanks in L.P.'s special—nay, world-esteemed—sauce. And the tide was flooding in on the breast of a fast-rising spring moon. Oh, yes! The gods and goddesses continued their ride through the heavens.

INCREDIBLE LIES

"I'm not sure what Mac's house rules are, but I think we should go along sooner rather than later in case things get uproarious. We can always fade out."

"Fine with me, but first two big cups of coffee for you. And I also want to drive through the elk refuge. This afternoon our post mistress told me that some trumpeter swans had settled in for a little R&R in the backwater near the weir. She thinks they came down from British Columbia."

Within minutes we were in the car. As usual, L.P. looked like a million bucks, American, which is just right. Just short of too much and never too little. The moon was flooding a burnished light soaring up from the peaks in the eastern sky.

"Let's turn right onto the old slough road and look for some elk on the way toward your club."

"*Our* club . . . ."

"It should be the elks club . . . but there's something else I've been meaning to talk to you about," said L.P.

Oh no, what was this? I panicked, narrowly missing a huge skunk sauntering along the curve of the dike road. His road.

"Shoot!"

"That's not a word to use in a federal game reserve, sweetheart."

"Well, spill it, then."

"Neither is that, in a world-famous estuary gleaming in the moon-light."

"Well, then, give me the skinny."

"I've been thinking that Dad used to make a special holiday cocktail very much the same as our Negroni, only he called it a Bronx; not quite so exotic as your new Florentine drink . . . or is it Venetian?"

Oh, man. Mamma mia!! And I had been agitated, worrying about something maybe serious.

A NECESSARY INTERLUDE

"Well, how about it?" How about a great sense of relief! A minor matter, but one never knows.

"How about it? You're right, as usual. An unlikely Manhattan bartender named Johnnie Solon at the old Waldorf Bar made it up of two-thirds Bombay Gin (100 proof), plus a dash of French and Italian vermouth and one-third orange juice. His odd concoction, named for his favorite borough. Frankly, it's almost the same, but not quite so robust; and to be even more frank, I prefer to associate your eye-opener with Count Negroni and his Venetian death wishes rather than the Bronx Zoo."

"What? A zoological garden?"

"That's right. He named it to honor the Bronx Zoo."

"And speaking of which," said L.P., "what am I looking at over there?" In the midst of an immense dusky moonlit savanna stood one of the largest deer herds I had ever seen. Then toward the center and quite separate from the encircling white-tailed deer, I could further see three or four dozen hulking male elk taking their ease, slowly feeding hock deep in the rich spring grass. A regular forest of Arden, calm and shimmering. I automatically decelerated to a glide. Their proud antlers rose and fell as they grazed and gazed.

"Let's not stop at night. The wardens get frantic when they see cars stopped near the game."

"Not to worry. We have our own herds to rendezvous with tonight." The moon was sending a long amber gold stairway cascading down the river, running in broad eddies beside us. What a sight! A ghostly ship with white bridgework had just turned the upriver bend, four miles away.

The vast breadth and intense gleam of the moonshine struck my wondering eyes; the sense of the faerie ring delineated by hooved animals in almost concentric, transmogrified, antic dances of fantastic antlered

INCREDIBLE LIES

imagery. We moved slowly through the shadowed scene, wishing that we were on foot, or at least on our bicycles. All was seemingly serenity and contentment. Reentering the old-growth rainforest provided another primal experience.

Beams splashed down, sparred moonglow. Meandering ditches and pools of water winked under the lunar light, thrusting up dazzling yellow spears of late-blooming skunk cabbage. Moss blankets swayed down from the hemlocks and stout alders. Magical, yes, but here and there just a shade too much sense of cypresses in the black lagoon in some long-forgotten backwater of southern Virginia. The range of the moon-splashed mossy greens beggared all writing. Nearing a watercress pool which boasted a secret hoard of wapato roots as well, L.P. suddenly squealed "some enchanted evening!"

Looking like an immense production of floating island desserts we could just see the rump feathers of roughly twenty trumpeter swans, bottom feeding in the moonlight. Lowering the windows we warbled the strains of *Swan Lake*, more or less. A full cast seemed to be in the pool, except the prince, his Black Swan, and of course evil Rothbart. Here a poacher would play his role, since there is a well-known secret, a ready, local palate for roasted swan.

One trophy bird floated in solitary rapture. A true Swan Queen. A Slavenska interpretation or perhaps Markova or even Margot Fonteyn. . . . While her courtiers fed, she preened.

I knew that this idyllic spell would remain legend with us always. Perhaps there would be other evenings of snowy cygnets and full moonlight, but it could never be quite the same. An Ondine experience.

"Remember the very first time we saw Fonteyn in *Sleeping Beauty*?"

"Of course," I responded quickly. "With Michael Somes . . . and Frederick Ashton."

"And Brian Shaw. Speaking of which I've seen no bluebirds here . . . yet."

"Magic it was, magic this is . . . but now we must press on. The herd instinct, don't you know."

"Yes, I know, but do you think other persons know the secret of these big birds?"

"Of course. They're protected now, and they've grown so strong even foxy Reynard thinks twice about approaching them. Those wings can break a leg."

"I'm sure that's what Leda said."

"What?"

"'Break a leg,' idiot. And you've obviously missed the goldfinches."

"Let's get on to the clubhouse before I begin to think about my English horn lessons. And we must find me a teacher!" Where, I wondered.

The main road was bathed in brimming light and I could just make out a black, low-slung county cruiser hunkered down beside a huge hassock of swamp grass edging the road. Ambush! We sailed sweetly by, a study in moonbeams at 55 m.p.h. We waved. He was wearing his big "smokes" to guard his night vision in the moonglow, no doubt.

In three minutes I was steering silently along the private gravel road to Firclad. A number of cars looked as though they had not moved since the morning tournament. They, too, gleamed in the moonlight, but there were no luminous reflections or flickering shadows. No animal mystery. But a whoop and some hollers came from the illuminated clubhouse windows. Happily, the home team had triumphed, but barely, and Mac's hole in one party was surely reaching some kind of hearty climax. An eventful weekend all around.

As we climbed from our car, a long shaft of moonbeam moved through the clouds and played up toward us from the slow swirling waters of the river far below. In some strange way known only to lunar beings, the light picked through an alder thicket beside our car. A hidden bed of trilliums and a bleeding heart glowed blood red and quiver white in a dark surround. L.P. was struck speechless by Mother Nature's bewitching moment of moonglow. Another memory etched forever, and most of it free!

"Greetings, lady fair" was the polished greeting from a too-steady Mac, filling in the light of his clubhouse entrance. "Welcome to this humble hall." Full of old world charm he was.

Oh, my, what a driveling line. L.P., however, was already lapping it up as we headed toward the buffet of smoked sturgeon and venison and bowls of dried cranberries . . . and what looked like jars of white lightning. I was invaded by thoughts of a robber's roost, some jolly outlaw band in a deep wood—MacRobin of Firclad. His lightning bolts packed authority.

L.P. was entranced, no doubt about it. I later heard something of her instant exchange with Mac. "I learned a great deal about you today, so I guess a little something about me is only proper." That was her opener.

"Oh, we know who you are, but the members have all voted you in." Another guffaw.

"But Mac, we've only been here a few months and our place is remote. You can't know much unless you talk to deer and loons."

"Well, we know. And after all, there are for interesting folks certain powers of deduction brought into play." The white lightning was obviously causing him no pain.

"Oh, really, Mac. Tell me about those powers."

"Well, Mrs. Vip, let me say first that in a county like ours no swallow falls that someone doesn't see it. Not much moves that there's not a report."

A NECESSARY INTERLUDE

"Oh, well, that's true everywhere. How about your powers of deduction? When do they come into play?"

L.P. said that Mac looked very intent and especially serious then, and to explicate he recalled a story about Sir Arthur Conan Doyle and profound secrets. He was transferring by Paris taxi from the Gare de Lyon to the Gare du Nord, on his way home from the Riviera.

"Thank you, Sir Arthur Conan Doyle," said the taxi driver on receiving his tip.

"How do you know who I am?" queried the writer.

"I saw in the papers that you were coming from Cannes by way of Marseilles. Your hair is cut in the Cannes style, and I observed Marseilles mud on your boots."

"Amazing, sir! Is this all you recognize me by?"

"No," was the driver's answer.

"There beside you I see your trunk with your name written in big letters."

Well, L.P. was smitten, especially when Mac said he knew all about me, too, and had been pulling my leg for two days. Well, maybe. Certainly he had made some phone calls. He didn't get it all from the swallows. They carried on all evening while I celebrated with my fellow members. Where the caviar came from I cannot tell.

Hours later, at least it seemed so, we were sedately cruising back down the river road toward home base.

"I loved meeting all our fellow members," chirruped L.P.

"Yes, they're a roisterous band, especially on a victory night. I'm not so certain there are that many of those."

"I think it was Mac's special night. Juanita certainly thought so. Sheer perfection . . . a hole in one. I can hardly wait for yours. . . ."

INCREDIBLE LIES

"Yes, but even in the heat of the recollection I was thinking about the swans. Remember that morning in 1968 when we were steaming through the narrows from Helsinki to Stockholm and you saw the flock of swans?"

"I'll never forget. After two months in Soviet Russia everything was enigmatic and inferential. I said they reminded me of all the doomed peoples under an evil Russian spell."

"That's what I was thinking about tonight in the clubhouse haze. Only I thought of the swans being various peoples in the different republics. They were held in an iron-ringed spell all these years by sorcerers, black magicians just like Rothbart—only the real thing. Who would ever have supposed?"

"And who can tell what will happen there next? I would never venture to say. When I looked over our Slavic collection the other night, half or more of the titles seemed passé. All those notions and complex analyses . . . all that grief."

We fell into pensive silence in the Slavic fashion and drove west. The moon was waning in the indigo sky. I refused to believe that dawn was coming, but then I sensed the low illumination from Astoria, the historic situation miles downstream where the sun did not rise.

We turned onto our road and saw the nocturnal hunting birds flap away as we sought our bed. What a day it had been: fishing, chopping, swinging the ax *and* the golf clubs.

And we had "seen the wool of the beaver and swan's down ever, and the bud of the briar and the bag of the bee," just as Ben Jonson said. How could so fine a day be so fairly and fully spent? Time must be set aside for savoring.

As we sank into bed the moon dipped down into Astoria . . . or was it Nagoya? . . . or Komoshita? They are building a golf course there, a links, though bordered by orange groves.

A NECESSARY INTERLUDE

The galaxy turned on its polar axis, and the next morning over steaming black coffee the review bubbled on.

"As I said on the way home, our new gang seems like a different cup of tea. At least to my untrained eye." L.P. flipped the eggs a yard in the air.

"Well, they are," I agreed. "I'm not certain what my dad would think thirty years later, not to mention his father."

"Did your grandfather play in New England? You never mentioned."

"Oh yes, more than a little, but not family outings. From the earliest club at Mont Royal in Montreal down through Maine and Massachusetts to Newport and St. Andrew's. I think he was in the playoffs at Sewickly and the Golf Club at Lakewood. I don't think St. Andrew's even exists any more. It was part of the Metropolitan Golf Association. The clubs had to be located on Long Island or within fifty-five miles of Manhattan. Those were the rules! Tuxedo Park was another, and maybe the best he thought was Wheaton. Then there was Onmentsia and Atlantic City."

I was busily mixing some B & Bs. Just enough. "The general idea was that players hit the ball between 170 and 190 yards in those days, and there could be one, two or three shots from the tee. Then, of course, there were the sand traps and water hazards of today, but the courses were simple. And so was almost everything else."

"And they were all private, I bet."

"Oh sure. These were tightly run, invitation-only clubs. That was simply understood . . . not even thought about. What else?"

"But the caddies could play."

"Yes, if the caddie master and greenskeeper had a good rapport with the membership. But emphatically not when any member was on the course. Or in the clubhouse either. Don't forget, we're talking the nineties and 1900. Some men like M.H. Harriman simply taught themselves to play, the way they learned stocks and bought whole countries. Straight ahead."

"That's incredible, really."

"Well, yes and no. My grandfather and father were simply well coordinated, essentially natural athletes."

"That's what I don't understand. You are too, except in the boat, but you've never had a hole in one. At least when we were together."

I lapsed into silence. Double eagles are better than the ace, in some ways.

I furthered some thoughts. "Harriman was a very strong, accurate player and a deadly putter, something like Findlay Davis. But maybe the main thing, L.P., is they subconsciously thought of themselves as gentlemen taking exercise, more or less in the British manner. And if they turned professional, well, that was that. It was no longer gentlemen's sport. At least not for a long generation. The larger number had learned the rules and the governing attitudes on the British courses. It's understandable, although a very distant past for us.

"I've seen all those photographs of the Gardiners, Hitchcocks, Winthrops, and Bayards. Those shoals of silver frames covering the pianos, conveying so much information, and so much . . ."

"I know what you mean," agreed L.P.

"I think my uncles had the best recollection of Gardiner Hubbard at Harvard; and John Reid, either Senior or Junior, who introduced the great game at Yale. I think Hubbard may have been self-taught, unlike you, L.P.; but what you're going to have in common with those long-ago players is style. You'll be a natural stylist, count on it."

I downed my drink, but L.P. was not quite ready.

"OK, I'll do my best. I want to do my best, and I will. You know that."

"I certainly do. So what's wrong?"

"And I wouldn't mind playing like Miss Rowland or Miss Terry. But if I ever have to wear mutton sleeves or a hat even remotely like Mrs. Fellowes

Morgan or the 1899 champion Ruth Underhill, you can count me out." Her glass went down, firmly.

I was nonplused. As usual, L.P. had been going into the matter thoroughly, much more than most. Like deep research. She didn't mention that most of their golf outfits looked like heavy duty bridal gowns. But I supposed that we would get into that in time.

THE SEVENTEENTH HOLE

My first conversation with Mac the next morning on the seventeenth tee is strong in my memory. Maybe it's a good thing that we had been delayed there. In truth, the stars in their courses might have dictated what unfolded in the next half-hour.

"For reasons that may ever elude me, this seventeenth hole appears to be my downfall. Maybe it's too clear-cut." This was unlike Mac, surely. Pros do not reveal chronic flaws.

"Well, I noticed there's only one trap on the far side, but the rough sure runs close to the green. And it's so thick. I could hardly walk through it yesterday."

"You seemed to be doing all right yesterday."

"I was, but now we have a kind of quartering wind. I just may use a two or three iron."

"It seemed yesterday like the five is your favorite."

"Well, it's true, I have a sentimental attachment."

The foursome ahead of us was still lolling about the green, three of them watching an unfortunate fourth stuck in the heavy, wet rough behind the green.

"Have you gone back to the five iron, Vip?"

I nodded uncertainly.

"That's not a five iron today. What's up?"

"Well, it's a long story, but very briefly, I traveled across Russia in the late sixties on the Trans-Siberian Railroad. It was a high-tension experience. Although political affairs were cold and glacial then, the three months changed my life. I was alone with lots of time to look around me and to think for long periods. Anyway, I talked it over with L.P. when we finally rendezvoused in our roach-infested room in the deluxe Moscow hotel where we were quartered for two cold-water weeks. Probably to distract her from all the little creatures running around the walls and across the floor, I proposed that we return and take our whole family across the Siberian line two summers later."

"Wow, what a trip! You must have had nothing but bucks for a trip like that. Also a professional guide, plus a bodyguard."

"Oh no! It just took a lot of nerve and a good credit rating. But the point of the story is that everyone was very careful and standoffish, maybe fearful. I wanted something special to attract attention. Let's call it a conversation piece, which would allow people to kind of ease up to ask us a question or two and strike up some kind of casual conversation. The train and station guards tried to prevent any contact with the locals. It was something I hadn't quite mastered until the end of my first trip."

"Clever idea."

"Right. The clever idea was a simple one. I chose a five iron and my brothers provided me with a large supply of golf balls."

"It's a great story."

"Actually, it is. Later I called it a 'bold tourney' as I put the first ball in the salt water off Diamond Head, one in the Emperor's moat in Tokyo, the carp pond of the world exposition at Osaka, into the Tsugaru Strait south of Hokkaido, and finally the heavily armed port of Nakhodka at American Bay. That's on the Siberian coast."

"Did you meet any Russian golfers?"

"Well, no. Among other things, Mac, you need golf courses before you can have players. Not to mention clubs, balls, gloves, tees, and a non-existent car to reach the non-existent course along a game path. In fact the only thing associated with golf that we saw was some kind of driving net on top of our own embassy in Moscow. The ambassador relieved his frustrations there, I've heard."

"Did your ploy work?"

"Oh yes. On the first trip people would scuttle up and ask one quick question. Did I know Tom Mix, or maybe Jeanette McDonald or Walt Disney or Jack London . . . ? I soon learned that the answer should always be yes. Even to J. Edgar Hoover."

"Why's that?"

"Well, they would look so sad and disappointed, and after all, you never want Slavs to be melancholy."

"So what would they ask?"

"Well, the first morning in Khabarovsk I was down on the beach pitching some balls across the Amur River toward China. They were kind of landing in the confluence of the Amur and the Ussuri rivers. So I was minding my own business when this delegation came along the beach toward me determined to ask two questions."

"Which were?"

"How much did I weigh . . . how much money did I make a year . . . and in a day . . . and were all those children ours? Yes was the answer, of course; and more directly asked: You must know Ike; you are his friend?"

THE SEVENTEENTH HOLE

Mac was intrigued, so I continued. "It was all so artless; I had a golf club. Ergo I was surely important. And who was the other important person they knew who played golf? Ike, of course.

"So I gravely replied yes each time. Nor was anyone in any way surprised or incredulous. They were all pleased and certain that my statement was fact. But wading up to their waists in the frigid river water of the Amur or later with the Lake Baikal delegation, our children were staggered. 'What a whopper!' they signaled, even Cameron at five. They almost forgot how cold the great Amur River waters were, surging northward past the straggling city and its bedraggled outskirts. They were too busy laughing at my whoppers. When I also dropped a good shot into Lake Baikal, that was good for some local chatter.

"Later in Irkutsk the local delegation reported to me with real sorrow that a golf course had almost been completed there (ha ha) in honor of Ike's proposed visit to the 'Paris of Siberia' . . . but then came the U-2 incident. Ike's Irkutsk landing was canceled. You remember that? Later in Moscow they said, 'Oh yes, your Gary Powers!' A golf setback. 'So unnecessary, so unfortunate,' said the military museum colonel-curator who was giving us a surprise showing of some carefully reconstructed U-2 air frame remains, without commentary. Powers' airplane parts were on view in museums all over the country. One answer to deconstructionism. If they had ever put all the so-called 'parts and fragments' together, the U-2 would have come out the size of a 747. Maybe he should have carried a wedge."

"What a moment! The high-flying U-2. What did you do?"

"I simply said, 'What's a U-2? Some new slang?' L.P., who knows all about high flyers, said rather airily, 'Colonel, I've never heard of it. I know us, too, and we two, but U-2 is new to us two.' L.P. was amused, but they were nonplused, especially since she delivers these remarks with an impeccable imperial accent. The delivery was also forceful, the imperative being the one presentation all attend to."

"What great sport, carrying the royal game right into the heart of the old evil empire!"

"That includes my long shot across the Ob, between Tomsk and Novosibirsk, one into the Volga at Kazan, and two over the Kremlin wall—after dark, of course. Night shots are never easy. For sentimental reasons I fired a Hagen Honey Center right over John Reed's memorial plaque, beside the wall. A shot that shook the world."

"That's a pre-war ball! Hagen Honey Centers are long gone."

"It should have shaken someone up. I distinctly heard glass shattering. Fortunately, we had drifted off around the corner of the famous GUM department store."

"What was the second ball you sent over?"

"Well, a K-2, of course. Or was it a K-28?"

"Aren't you the one, I mean really! Let's get on with this game while those guys ahead of us have their backs turned. Besides, the wind is dropping. That's a favor."

"Good thought. I hate spectators. But then I knocked one over the wall at Elsinore, for Hamlet; one into the Zuider Zee; and then the Seine, near the Eiffel Tower."

Mac's eyes grew ever wider. He had asked for it, so I plowed on. "Later we crossed the Channel and stayed in an inn beneath Dover Castle. The children built their own town on the strand, and since the tide was at low ebb I laid down several iron shots along the sand while L.P. read 'Dover Beach.' Matthew Arnold would have loved it. He believed in games, you know. He never mentioned golf, but then neither did Queen Victoria. Things caved in for some time when the Hanoverians arrived in London. Appropriately, they enjoyed boar hunting."

"Okay. So how about London?" said Mac, giving in, or maybe out.

"As I remember I confined myself to Green Park, in deference to the memory of the first Duke of Wellington. He was a sportsman, but I think no golfer; however, he was the ranger of Green Park, among a thousand honors. He allowed some practice shots there. Golf, I mean. His Scottish generals played."

"How about Hyde Park?"

"Oh, I played at 7:00 on Sunday morning when the gates opened, then we went over to the Ritz for a special brunch. Some things should be done once." Later I would tell Mac about the Battery on Manhattan, the "green" at Lexington, and my last shot at Concord Bridge . . . in honor of the American volley "heard round the world."

I had never talked so much or so rapidly. Silence now seemed best. Mac was studying the seventeenth hole as though he had never seen it before, looking down toward the green and the surrounding stand of firs and alder as though for the first time. Suddenly he turned and walked toward me.

"This is ridiculous. I shouldn't be teeing off first. When I was thinking back over the holes I suddenly realized it's your honor. You won the last hole, so you're one up on me in match play!" This also seemed ridiculous, if not impossible.

But maybe I was. Such niceties were never a big deal with me, especially in a twosome. There was no money involved, which seems to be the reason some guys play golf—and women, too, if you can believe it. Anyway, I said okay and decided on a four iron, the wind being what it was, fickle. I changed to a three.

That was an immediate and obviously terrible mistake. A huge clump of blackberry vines had somewhat screened us from a hard wind at our backs, and I really misjudged the velocity of the winds above us. My ball flew across the green, high above it in fact, showing the slight hook also favored by my younger brothers.

Hitting a thick alder tree behind the green with a hard crack, the maddened ball then came back across the green, bouncing twice and rolling over the apron and down into an obviously deep pit in front of the green, a bunker in the Scottish manner. In fact it reminded me of the celebrated "Road Hole" at old St. Andrew's . . . the seventeenth of blackest notoriety.

· · · ·

A few years before I had walked over that legendary course by invitation one late fall day. Of particular interest to me was one incomparable hole, for it was there that my next older brother just days before the well-televised 1978 British Open had triumphed in a special way. Throughout the tournament, several great players had somehow foundered and crashed at the infamous Road Hole. Tailspinned, power-dived . . . you name it. The bedeviled seventeenth had claimed a phalanx of proud players. Daniel had been among the tournament spectators and had stared in meditative silence down into the deep den beside the seventeenth green.

The next day he had played with a couple of Americans and an especially dashing New Zealand squadron commander yearning for a pick-up game. Danny's grizzled caddie mentored and kibitzed him around the course. He reported things went reasonably well until the famous Road Hole and its blind tee shot. There he finally connected and hit a long hook, beyond his norm, through rough grass and onto the fairway. The caddie expelled a cloud of smoke and thought very hard. He was just out of sight of the far-off flag, although the green was in view of a keen eye.

At this point his ancient caddie came wide awake. Scrutinizing the hole, and then my brother and his size, he said, "You can shoot right over yon point, doctor, and put that little ball right next to the flag. They've just replaced it square in the middle of the green. So do it, if you please."

What amazing advice, thought my brother. "Just how do you propose I do this, caddie? I don't even know where the infamous green is from here, except from newsreels."

"Yes, I know that, sir, but see yon spires there on the kirk? Shoot straight at them with a slight hook, and not too high; but neither should it be too low. Long and slow, sir. A fast ball will roll right on and then off the green and maybe into the pit," he brooded. It may have been an unnecessary remark, but also a forewarning. More smoke went down.

Abandoning everything but concentration, Daniel blasted a ball at the church, an indeterminate distance away. The caddie nodded with deep satisfaction, exhaling blue-black tobacco smoke from places down around his ankles.

Moving over the hill toward the elusive green, the steadfast and loyal ball could then be seen cheek side to the flag. And a number of townsfolk were gathering by the low stone wall which guards the town from the hole, or vice versa. Without a thought for consequence Daniel simply walked up and tapped his ball into the cup. There was a burst of applause from the onlookers. His struggling partners were equally enthusiastic, but near speechless.

INCREDIBLE LIES

"A birdie," breathed the gnarled caddie, thinking of his fine rewards so rightfully earned. "The only birdie this whole year," declared a townsman. "And what a masterful second shot!" exclaimed another. "Last week, sir, Arnold Palmer marked down a seven twice on this treacherous hole," offered the butcher. Daniel had been in a trance.

Yes, 1978 was a vintage year for my brothers at play.

. . . .

I again pulled back from my Scottish reverie as the foursome ahead of us moved with a contented rhythm borne of a life generally spent out of doors. I had learned yesterday that Firclad had its own pits.

"Speaking of balls, though, I'm down to my last one, and it has a big hack in it for some reason or other." How could a pro run short of balls? I puzzled over something that simply never happens. Shouldn't happen. But Mac was nothing if not a surprise in full, uninhibited bloom.

"Here, I've got plenty," said I rifling in my bag. It was then that I pulled out the long gray feather with a slight white trim. How it had escaped my short memory is hard to say; but there it was, a good foot and a half long, and in perfect condition . . . and one small tip.

"Well, well. Look what you've got there, eagle feathers . . . and how come you're packing these somewhat illegal things around?"

I told Mac about my experience beneath the sheltering fir the day before, while I was waiting for inspiration on the sixth fairway.

Without giving it much more thought I then smoothed the gray plumage, turned away and muttered a spontaneous incantation to our grand national bird. Facing me was a long slope of rippling meadow grass which fell away from the backside of the small, heavily pockmarked seventeenth tee. Down in the bright mint sedge of a water track I could just make out a long green swirl of yellow blossoming wild water iris which some long-ago flight of birds had carried to the hillside pond. And even more I could just make out an astonishingly long natural dam which some family of beavers were continuing to extend, in this case to some farmers' delight. An amorous pair of wood ducks settled into a small alder grove beside the pond, momentarily interrupting the furry meal of a sleek marten patrolling the banks of the natural reservoir. Water was abundant wherever I cast my eyes. A verdant landscape.

When I turned back toward Mac, I sensed something special in the air. He seemed wholly in the grip of a mood far beyond what I had taken to be his come-what-may approach to the great game and to life in general. Seemingly under my slouchy influence, he had obviously decided against his usual one practice swing, and now he had at last chosen a three iron in the face of the fickle wind. I was amazed. He was surely over-clubbed for 169 yards.

"I just can't get over your eagle feathers," he muttered.

Single eagle versus double eagle. He took his time teeing up, gazing way off into space and then far down at the flag standing straight out in the wind. "Preoccupied" would best describe Mac, but he continued his studied preparations.

"We sometimes forget that eagles also have shoulders, elbows, wrists, and even hands," he offered from his crouch. I was looking just a little transfixed by his sudden aside, I'm sure, enamored as L.P. and I are of the great national bird. Mac was obviously informed, hardly surprising.

"I'd guess what you have there is a leading feather, something all our Plains Indians treasured. We know it as a primary remigis or an under major primary covert, or just possibly an under median covert." I realized he was way into technical talk about bird flight.

"We do?" This long soar through arcane matters was already far over my head. What next? Wait until L.P. heard about this! Raptors were her long-standing passion. That was one of several nicknames she gave me, truth to be known. Careless Raptor.

"Well, this is something special then, Mac. As far as I'm concerned, this exceptional artifact of flight holds mystical powers associated with speed and accuracy in long-distance journeys." My memory then is that of a sudden moment. Fleeting.

The main thing is that the green ahead was again clear of players and it suddenly took on an intense, more green than green, dramatic look, highlighted by a long brilliant shaft of sunlight which broke through the clouds and spilled over the ragged putting surface. The modest hole was transformed by refracted Newtonian lights playing across the gritty green and turning the scene into a world class golf experience, excepting of course my own ball in the pit. The flag fluttered like a turret banner at Hollyrood or Tintagel.

Mac did not just perform his effortless, southpaw magic. He was coiled and seemed in a transfixed state as he lashed at his teed-up ball. Off it sped, spring-loaded, as though fired from a long rifle with great speed and low trajectory. Too low, oh yes! But at high velocity. The ball just caught the lip of my pit and sped on nearly undeflected, a long yard above the green.

We then distinctly saw and then heard Mac's ball whack the pin, shuddering in the wind. We saw—*everyone* saw—his ball drop like a felled ox, or Galileo's stone, falling straight down the pin, burrowing into the hole like a rabbit. No nonsense. It simply dropped out of sight.

THE SEVENTEENTH HOLE

A dead calm fell over the links. It would seem that players on at least half a dozen tees and fairways witnessed Mac's truly odd shot and very splendid moment. An exultant howl of shared ecstasy began to rise from fifty throats. Later, people said I was surely carried away by the moment because I tossed him in the air. But Mac and I distinctly observed a huge flock of wild pigeons wheel and turn to circle once over the flag . . . several times in domino convolutions. Celebratory.

Mac stood in a catatonic state, the improbable three iron resting on his knobby shoulder. What a moment—a very long, pleasurable, timeless moment. He continued to stand motionless, incredulous.

"Mac, what a moment for you! What can I say? How about . . . happy anniversary? What a perfect gift!"

"It can't be. Not on this hole. Not with this club! My God, what will people around here say?"

"They'll want to cheer and crow with you."

"They'll crow, all right, when they learn I was using a three iron. I don't even know how I picked that club. And the ball! It should have gone into the next county . . . into the ocean."

"Mac, you only met me yesterday, but let me tell you there are a few things I do perfectly well, and one of them is keep secrets . . . forever." I did not mention my personal diary, which is the best-kept secret. "So you had a four iron, or maybe a five."

I picked up my bag and Mac got into his cart, slowly motoring toward the green among a gathering band of exuberant friends clapping and cheering his rite of passage from virgin player to full maturity. The ace! The cheering reached a crescendo as he faultlessly drew my lucky Titleist from the hole and entered a one on his card. The milling crowd shook Mac's hand and slowly, mercifully, moved back toward their own games. Five agonizing strokes later I was out of the foul pit, a trap that must certainly be far deeper as a result of my thrashing. Mac marked a seven next to my name and said there was no sand left in the trap and would I order a truckload.

But who could care? Mine was a non-event. Mac had lived through a perfect moment.

No one could believe his wiliness, his cunning; how in the face of what was by now in the telling a forty-mile wind (sorry about that, Admiral Beaufort), Mac had suddenly remembered an old mid-iron trick and yanked out a long shafted three iron as in the days of old on some wind-blown links on a Scottish seaside. But the real secret was safe, the flight of the eagle's feather . . . and my muttered prayer. That was a VPP secret.

As we strolled toward the eighteenth tee, leaving his cart on the tree-bordered walk, Mac spoke as from a deep fog.

"I have a further secret, Vip, and you're the only one who will ever know."

We unconsciously moved closer together. Oh, for my diary!

"Do you remember my back was to you on the tee?"

"Yes, I remember; no practice swing."

"Oh, that . . . By George, I don't even remember! But just as I was ready to swing I suddenly changed my whole grip. Up until I was fifteen I used an interlocking finger grip which my dad finally broke me of, thank heavens."

"Oh I remember it well . . . . So did my dad."

"Well, just as I was ready to play, my hands suddenly found their way back into the old grip . . . really almost by themselves."

Magic fingers, I mused. Yes, the perfect phrase, with emphasis on the magic. But not to become a habit, of course.

THE SEVENTEENTH HOLE

I would be hard put to describe my elation over Mac's great feat. I was involved in every aspect of it from the moment he had teed up. In a sense I felt as if I had somehow made the hole in one myself, silly as it seems, with the same ball, of course. Anyway, Mac was bursting with quiet pride in a somehow inner glowing way. It couldn't be faulted. He was silent, but savoring. After all, it was *the* moment, one I'd never experienced and probably wouldn't at the rate I was progressing. But how silly! Who was to say? Who knows what lies down the road? Any road. We can only look so far, happily.

THE EIGHTEENTH HOLE

Mac was in a transcendent non-virginal state, but he did agree we had to finish out the ninth, which is to say his eighteenth. While he joshed with yet another foursome of chortling friends drifting by, I took the bull by the horns and teed off. Strictly speaking, protocol-wise, I erred, but we did have to get in and tell Mrs. Mac, though Juanita probably had heard by now anyway. Such news makes its own way at light speed.

Not thinking about anything in particular except the cruelly hidden green some 512 yards out of sight, the unpredictable happened. Clean and effortlessly, I hit one of the strongest drives of my curiously long life. A couple of Mac's cronies gaped, but I carefully said nothing. Why reveal astonishment? There was no loud crack; everything simply fused into motion, so easy that I put it out of my mind.

With another round of congratulatory whoops, Mac's admirers trudged off to their carts and he centered one straight down the middle, over the crown of the first hill. No drive was long enough on this hole, especially the way it was set up as the eighteenth. Hidden fairways and greens are a bother. One should ordinarily be able to savor the approach, the surround of each green as one walks toward it. Golf is more than part theater, as players would attest.

We strolled along, drinking in every pleasure his triumph afforded. All things seemed to flourish wherever we turned our eyes; truly, as in Pope's *Windsor Forest*. But Mac then turned off to get his cart while I reflected over golf architecture, something about this long hole and our basic family antipathy to hidden greens. It's the true mark of an American golfer. Personally, I don't care how shaggy and hilly the course is. In fact I prefer the craggy hillock and sea dune links; but I also prefer to see the green somewhere ahead of me, or to know a dogleg is in the cards—whatever the breed. The pleasure of anticipation rather than of surprise.

So far as I could tell, Mac had pulled a brassie from his bag, but I hadn't even seen my ball as yet. He appeared to have sliced along the right-hand margin in some medium rough grass which held his second shot on the high slope. From that vantage point he motioned to me that my ball had some- how gone on along over the second hill. And, wondrously, so it had. Fortunately it skirted the windrows of fallen trees lining the rough.

As I moved across the crest, puffing just the barest, I could just see it crouched down behind a bit of early plantain. Not a good spot by any means, plus a downhill lie. But what distance! A drive over 350 yards. I pulled my lip. Mrs. Mac had come out of her tiny clubhouse kitchen and was watching our final approach, drying her big strong hands on the world's largest apron. She must have heard.

"Don't forget, we're still with winter rules," said Mac.

"You can move it six inches from where you are, which looks to me like some kind of baby gopher hole."

"I'm taking you up on that, Mac, because I want to get close to the green."

"Why don't you just get on the green?" he urged. "Never up, never in!"

"In this wind? Who're you kidding!" My thoughts had instantly gone to the Master. Roughly speaking, he said that nine-tenths of all golfers quail at the thought of a headwind. I could clearly recall his advice: treat the wind as part of the golf course, and then add twenty yards to the shot. If I had owned one of those new little hand-held devices, I could have measured very closely; but my own eye told me that the flag at the back of the elevated green, hunched in to the hillside, was about 112 yards away; plus the Master's twenty, call it 138 yards, certainly fewer than 140. But then the bloody wind was rising . . . Bobby had also said that a player must be quiet and calm. Then, too, there was the downhill lie, and the grim details of gravity and mass. One's body weight against the slope. All those canted muscles. But then I could not recall what he wrote about that. I voted for confidence and serenity and a little prayer. After all, Mrs. Mac was watching too. Then, too, I was a gray panther . . . really gray.

And then, what club? As though in a trance, I reached in the old canvas sack and pulled out the wedge. I had never owned one before, but then neither had phlegmatic Johnny McDermott. It seemed somehow a desperate remedy. What a laugh; it laid into my hand like a Churchill shotgun. The perfect weight, the perfect grip, the perfect length. As I struck the ball I recalled Stewart Maiden's superb one-line telegram to Jones in 1919: "Hit 'em hard. They'll land somewhere."

Madness must have seized me, because I quickly hit the ball very firmly without even thinking or concentrating in any way. My Titleist flew in the air. Oh, so high! I was afraid it would hit the clubhouse, one of my specialties. But it didn't! It flew from my clean slash straight to the green. It stood in the wind for a hovering moment. Like a sparrow hawk. Then it stooped toward the green. It bounced. Good Lord, it bounced three times

THE EIGHTEENTH HOLE

and rolled out of sight. I was sure it was in the hole! Don't ask me how I knew. "Great Caesar's ghost, Mac, I think I just made an eagle."

"What do you mean?" he crowed. "How can you do this to me in my own moment of ecstasy? You've just shot a double eagle."

"Well, yes, but it's not a hole in one. You had that."

"That's right. It's not an ace, I know, but let me tell you, it's better than an ace. Look at Juanita waving her apron. She knows it's in the hole."

"Who will believe this? Your hole in one followed by my double eagle. But not a hole in one for me."

We rested on the hillside while he expounded. "You don't seem to understand. A double eagle is indubitably more demanding than a hole in one. You need to hit two very long shots sequentially and perfectly; and the second one can't be teed up artificially."

"Well, maybe we should check."

"Oh, it's in there, all right. Look at that big apron flapping away."

"Who would believe it?"

"Well, I for one. First of all, this has got me thinking; and I now know who you really are. This kind of golf runs in your family . . . well, part of it does, let's say. You see, I know your brother Dick."

"You do? How so?"

"Of course. Everyone who has played a few greens has heard about his record: four double eagles, the first and second holes at Inglewood in Seattle; the 510-yard tenth at Portland Golf Club; and then the 501-yard eighteenth hole at the great Broadmoor course. So now we both know."

"As a matter of fact, Mac, I've never had the details. He's taciturn. But it sounds about right. I know that he's been on those courses through the years. The hard part, though, is his nonchalance. He shrugs it off. *Savoir faire*, you know. Of course some par fives are tougher than others, but there's no doubt he has the world record on this. Unrecorded, of course. He should get those witnesses still hobbling around, especially the 475-yard uphill fairways at Inglewood. They are all legitimate double-eagle holes."

"Oh, don't worry. Lots of people have heard, and I sure know that he has; and what's more, a double eagle is far smarter golf because you don't have to buy drinks for the house. A hole in one can be at once a source of pride and a financial disaster. And, of course, we all love eagles. But those holes I mentioned are all tough, legitimate par fives. But back to your ace."

"Well, let's hope a lot of players have already gone home. After all, our team won, and no visitors will be hanging around to gloat."

"That's a break. But I'll gladly pay, except for you. That would be too much. All that modesty and humble notions. You've humbugged me!"

"That's just what the Duke of Wellington said," I exclaimed; but I could see that he was honestly amused.

As we climbed the sharp side of the approach to the eighteenth, the sudden blaze of sunlight bursting out of the scudding clouds was a theatrical finish, with no crowds, no cameras, and no commentators. Except for Mrs. Mac, who was trilling with delight. The perfect crowd, to my way of thinking—that of a very private person.

"I was standing right there," she exclaimed. "Your ball simply dropped out of the clouds and bounced in the hole!"

My response was a foolish grin. As I strolled across the green she said, "But aren't you excited? You got an eagle!"

As I gathered up my ball from the truly narrow cup, two swift shadows sped across the green. This was the vaunted sign. Two eagles in tandem, to match mine.

THE EIGHTEENTH HOLE

"Hey, Juanita! Vip got a double eagle! That was his drive back there!"

Then I looked up toward the northwest. How lucky could I be? The now familiar eagles were gliding off toward the ocean-bound hills. Another double. I always thought that was only in band music. But then I turned to Mrs. Mac and said, "Yes, my first double eagle ever. But listen, there's a much finer and shorter tale to tell. The real story!"

Mac's Juanita looked ever more radiant and flushed with wonderment as I began to tell the tale of her jaunty husband's flawless ace. All the sophistications of golf aside, there is nothing so magical as that penultimate moment, the hole in one. Every player knows that's what makes all the eagles scream.

The tale told, Mac and Mrs. Mac went toward the clubhouse arm in arm. Such a moment! And I was tempted to follow; however, this was simply not possible. It was imperative in the canons of golf that one of us finish the theoretical nine, otherwise we might inherit Sam Snead's luck. So I strolled off toward the first four fairways, which double with somewhat different tees as the tenth through thirteenth holes. I was once more a truly private person, the lonely player as a "romantick." Besides I had my double eagle to keep me warm, even though it wasn't the ace.

THE TENTH HOLE

As I teed up I reviewed the simple fact that playing from this same tee the preceding day, fate had awarded me another eagle. What a weekend! Okay, so Firclad was too easy. But who else had shot my score . . . at least on some holes? Simply speaking, it was life-enhancing.

With that elation flooding through me I hit two wonderfully long successive drives well over 260 yards and far, very far out in the brooding fir trees. What absurdity! The price of carelessness. Or was it fatigue? It was now a long afternoon, slump time. And after all, I was also a very private, increasingly senior citizen. That useless thought had to be shaken off. Concentrate on golf and only golf! I dug for another ball, my third drive.

I pronated my wrists in the mysterious fashion of Ben Hogan and struck gold; straight down the middle. And I mean straight, through a small alder clump rearing up right in the center of the fairway. I am not keen about mid-fairway obstacles which thwart a truly stroked shot. Near my ball a coyote darted from the undergrowth, slinking east. On the other hand my irritation was aimless and academic. The gods had pushed me through some amazing moments of golf. As I stalked down the grassy slopes I suddenly thought along another line. The coyote's howl accompanied me.

Of all the players I had seen in two days, only Mac, part-time, and I and Brawn and his Herculean partner were walking. Everyone, but everyone, was in a golf cart. Sometimes two to a cart, but most often four carts! That's a lot of wear and tear on any course, and oh so much horsepower and less manpower. I needn't get too worried about such developments, but I did ask myself what would the Duke of York have thought, not to mention suave Charles himself. They were sportsmen, day and night. It had never occurred to them to have servants and sedan chairs on their seventeenth-century fairways. Both were monarchs as well as sportsmen, and they had walked, as did George V, Edward VIII, and George VI, and Walter Hagen, and my own father. One of my perverse friends said, "Golf simply spoils a pleasant walk," but my dad knew the measured walk was part of the rhythm of God's greatest game.

Down toward the out of bounds fence, which my first two drives had cleared by many yards, an unbelievably large clump of beautiful sword fern was emerging from the wet, growing before my eyes. I even heard a bullfrog croak from the morass. It truly was spring. I bounced along the turf, continuing my musing, listening for a nightingale or cuckoo. Obviously I was in the wrong region for such sounds.

But for me much of the release and infinite promise of golf was simply walking along the grassy vistas and scrambling a bit in the rough hillsides—the slopes and crags each course should have if not established beside the surf or on the strand of a loch, a firth or wild shore. That random thought suddenly routed my backward thinking toward one of my last great outings of long ago, before courses were tamed and hemmed in by housing and artful developers and big name players.

In 1946, as a kind of reunion after warfare, my brothers had laid out a long week of golf playing upcountry from northern California to Seattle. Four of us were pretty much home from the wars, and our youngest brother would soon be en route across the Pacific toward what would explode into the ill-starred "Korean Crisis."

But first things first, we decided; some rounds of golf on favorite courses to include gifted Chandler Egan's re-styled Pebble Beach, the Olympic, the notable courses in Medford and Eugene, then over to Seaside and Gearhart on the north Oregon coast. The Seaside links was unknowingly laid out in the midst of a pre-history native village. I was especially keen about Gearhart, a very fine old course in the national record book, one where the explorers Lewis and Clark had earlier walked, subconsciously, I was almost certain, laying out the tenth and eleventh fairways of today. No doubt! Then on to the rich deep turf of Astoria Country Club and its wind-filled labyrinths. The eighteenth hole at Astoria, over five hundred yards and a dazzling distilled water hazard and lazy dogleg, should rank among the great holes in the golfing universe. Almost as Sacagawea and William Clark first saw it. Every beauty of the far western shore is realized there, especially on a mid-summer morning.

From there to the beautiful Waverley and Alderwood clubs in Portland, and to the lush new nine holes making up the "eighteen" at Longview. Finally by unanimous decree—in fact there was no vote at all—our youngest brother Gerry was delegated to lay out a rough mountain scramble along the sides of our favorite volcanic peak in southern Washington, Mount St. Helens. The grand finale. Seattle and underrated Tacoma would come later as dessert. After all, the grand old

Tacoma Golf Club was older than any California upstart—not to mention Seattle.

Since he had actually been born in a clubhouse and in essence was "to the manner born," Gerry was given the most entertaining but demanding assignment in our odyssey. Gerry had taken some special time devising nine hair-raising alpine holes established at around 8,500 feet, with lots of moss, huckleberries, and rocks, but no grass. There were to be even two or three natural water hazards—hot water, of course! As it happened, "unnatural" would have better described them. But I digress.

We had first stayed at the newly founded Marines' Memorial Club in San Francisco, and then very early on a Monday morning in August we arrived for an 8:00 tee off time at unvexed Pebble Beach, where Dan had several times played the "public course" in the California State Amateur. Those were Elysian days. We gazed through empyrean calm at the master work of Douglas Grant of dear old Yale and the inspired insights of Jack Neville—the great amateurs who preceded Egan in laying out Pebble Beach.

Daniel was well connected at Del Monte even then, and since the course was empty and no one scheduled for play until 10:00, we were cheerfully sent off as a fivesome by ever-obliging Ray Parco, the legendary caddie master. Daniel observed, somewhat grandly, that he could not under any circumstances arrange this kind of irregularity at Cypress Point. Nonetheless, he would try.

It was a life-enhancing kind of day, not a cloud in the sky, no wind other than cooling zephyrs. Everyone played well, with one exception, me. That is, except for the sixth and seventeenth holes. Having erratically visited every part of the renowned golf course and actually missed the ball at least half a dozen times, I put the fear of the Lord into my partners twice, which is much better than nothing, I say.

On the long sixth I was on the green in two against a quartering wind, but on the seventh, two very well-hit nine iron shots simply flew over the green into the ocean beyond. On the sixteenth (390 yards) my ball rolled over the renowned kidney shaped green and rabbited into the sand pit beyond. I simply couldn't get out. Yet on the seventeenth my tee shot was just inches from the flag! Alas, there was not a soul around the brilliant hole to see my birdie. Other than my thunderstruck partners, that is. I remember every stride in the 180 yards.

We rounded out well on the fabled eighteenth, realizing full well that we were at our height on maybe the hole of greatest fame, trying to look like classy Chandler Egan on the greatest linkside hole ever. Since it never happened again, I like to think that we brought it off. On occasion, press home.

. . . .

My new obsession, Firclad, certainly did cause my mind to look back through time's flight . . . and much more. And it gave me much pleasure to look back, even in detail.

Looking farther along the forest lining on the left flank of the long first (tenth) fairway, two things suddenly came to mind. One was that I must be in the chips at last, because I had made a perhaps small, but nonetheless significant purchase on Friday without thought or hesitation. My whole life had slowly played out with never, ever, a single purchase of golf tees. They had always been available to gleaners, casually searching the front of most teeing areas, even in the 1930s. Occasionally they could even be found in the fairways (yes, shocking to say), especially on long yardage holes . . . but my casual purchase of a package of ten for a dollar had taken place without a flinch. Yes, times were good! But plastic tees were a no-no. A short-lived introduction, cursed by the mower sharpeners.

Then, too, there no longer seemed to be any sand boxes for the cleverly constructed sand tees of early days, except on the first tee. Nor were there any ball washers in evidence, with those brisk, churn-like handles and water-soaked brushes to brighten up a hard-used ball. And no towels.

The other thing I noted with some long-time interest was my seemingly offhand attitude toward crows. I usually paid far too much attention to the wily birds and their raucous cries, whether in the wilds of a city park in as dense a situation as Manhattan's Central or Green Park in London, at the top of Athabasca Pass in the Canadian Rockies, or the ocean forest along Gray's Harbor. Suddenly on the branches of the fir forest I could see a rough thousand congregated. They were holding a spring convention, but the wind baffled their noisy meeting.

THE ELEVENTH HOLE

Looking at the beautiful "eleventh," which had caused me such astonishment as the second hole the preceding day, I pondered. Everything looked much the same. If possible, the looming dogwood looked even more beautiful. A certain tension was absent. I knew that Lucky Pierre's was on a far-off slope with his several new responsibilities. To increase and multiply is never simple, so he was tied up.

Furthermore, though Lucky was gone, today's wind had returned with greater force. Two sharp memories then jogged my solitary reflections as I followed after my caromed drive. The wind had served me well, holding the ball on the edge of the fairway just out of the dense stands of pussy willows. Better than the preceding hole anyway. But again my mind was snared by the tricky chasms of the Lincoln green Astoria Country Club, most especially the unpredictable eighteenth hole which our memorable "tour" had played.

· · · ·

For reasons that as usual defy analysis, I was stuck on that hole, actually right through the gizzard. The hole has a slight dogleg turn running endlessly to the left. Until then, on the fairways at least, I had been, albeit some-what lamely, keeping up with my family fivesome. But on that, one of the several demanding holes at Astoria, I almost customarily teed off last. The wind was seen to take my well-struck ball and actually carry it back toward our tee. So I was first to hit a second shot, which was also wafted back from the bend in the fairway.

My third shot, which was also well-played, put me in perfect position for a long two iron to the green. The other four were preparing their plans for their second strokes to the green. Just as I struck my ball, again very well, the fickle wind reversed itself and actually carried my ball high over the green into the beckoning slough. The mysteries of Beaufort's scale would have been unavailing, had I been aware of them then. My second ball landed square on the green with a perfect five iron, which club my four brothers used, except for Dick, who naturally thought a six iron would do. And it did, for him. But foxy John won the hole and the match, pitching in from seventy yards, a shot almost duplicating one he had made at thirteen to win the "Tiny Tads" championship in Washington state.

My second memory had to do with learning Admiral Beaufort's useful practical scale of wind velocities. By the remotest chance years ago, I had been given a sudden and unexpected chance to look over an arcane archive in the Orkney Islands. L.P. thought the whole idea was enchanting. We were very young and enthusiastic about everything and less than forty-eight hours notice to sail to the U.K. meant nothing. Doesn't everyone drop everything to sail the Atlantic?

It was only just after the war, and when we walked ashore at Liverpool after a high-speed uneventful voyage from New York, we were frankly shocked. The grand and commodious seaport capital so revered by Henry James and other trans-Atlantic travelers looked worn out. The city hall made a remarkable impression on L.P. Hard service through two convulsive wars, however, had given every pier, every landing shed and goods wharf an exhausted, battered appearance.

There hadn't been many travelers on our eastbound North Atlantic passage. In the face of all the obvious distress, I felt strangely embarrassed as we followed an ancient porter sedately moving our luggage and typewriters a long half-mile. My golf clubs, which I had impetuously thrown in the Manhattan taxi at the last moment, suddenly seemed out of place on my shoulder. This was no place or time for play. The cavernous, bomb-blasted Liverpool passenger station was dimly lit, and those few persons about appeared as careworn as the buildings about them. Brave, but truly tired out, was the theme. Then the porter said, "Well, governor, I'm glad to see the old golf sticks coming back again." I gulped and paid handsomely. British porters have a dependable style.

We purposefully moved on by rail toward our Manchester connection, bypassing glorious old Chester with much reluctance. We had to change trains in bomb-pocked Manchester, actually walking with a porter in attendance between what appeared to be the station depots of two different railroads about a mile and a half apart. But it was easily done, and certainly not the curdling experience of twenty years later, finding our way about and through the nine railroad stations serving Moscow with four children and heaps of luggage in tow.

Happily the tired but well-kept old train then took us a long way around, through densely packed and grimly determined Leeds. From the evening train we later spied a majestic glow in the brilliant sun which appeared for one long minute as the huge ball dropped from the cloud cover toward the immediate horizon. What we saw from our speeding train were the hulking towers of the Venerable Bede's Durham Cathedral;

vast, unharmed and invincible. An ennobling inspiration through centuries of strife.

Our late-night arrival in Edinburgh was greeted at last by a pleased night clerk at the Roxburghe, who commented on our long journey "to the golf links." No one had commented on my clubs since the boat shed, but the hotelier quite naturally assumed we were on our way to St. Andrews. Truth to be told, L.P. and I had not discussed my last-minute decision. The clubs had simply appeared like Excalibur, roughly speaking.

By lucky chance our northbound morning train took the undulating coast route out of Waverley Station. Crawling over the timeless wonders of the Firth Bridge we could see a vast gathering of mostly British warships anchored off the naval yard and ancient keep at Rosyth. Most of the faded shadows of camouflaged ships now idly swinging at their moorage revealed years of hard service in the world's oceans. L.P. commented on the great battle fleets and their commanders of two wars, such as Jellicoe, Madden, Beatty, Tyrwhitt, Pound, Tovey, Cunningham, Fraser, and Somerville. She had scarcely begun. Each had moved ponderous armadas past the steel towers of the cantilevered bridge. She seemed to know them all through the two world wars, which, as usual, was no surprise to me. Even Sturdee, Arbuthnot and Horton.

For some reason of continuing bomb repair, our slow-moving train was shunted off the Dundee track, luckily moving off toward the thirty-odd sea miles of tidal landscape below St. Andrews . . . and of course, the picturesque and timeless mecca, The Royal and Ancient Golf Club. The weather was perfect, with a clear, fast-rising sun, something Admiral Jellicoe would have died for at Jutland, just across the North Sea. As we approached the old royal burgh. I could see far off some stout-hearted bathers taking a late dip in the already wind-tossed beach surf.

As we rattled past the jumble of lodging and hotels along the track and around the station, the train attendants bustled to help us. They naturally assumed that we were bound for the revered "Autumn Meeting," for many years postponed at the Royal and Ancient Club. But I waved them off, to their surprise.

"Are you bound for Carnoustie, then?" said the ticket taker.

"Not this year, unfortunately. We have our clubs, but it has to be business first this year."

"Well, Carnoustie has been well-nigh abandoned since 1939 and the Huns; but so have the links here. But Carnoustie, now, is truly a bonny course."

"Aye," said the arriving conductor, eyes gleaming. "Carnoustie should also have its royal title. With a fine sea headwind, the sixth hole stands above all others in that most brutal clutch of holes." He was already waxing.

"You're forgetting the world-esteemed seventeenth and eighteenth. Many's the fine player who's gone to destruction on Barry Burn." L.P. and I were long forgotten in this memory game of links battles lost and won. The train crew were in their element.

"We're heading north, beyond Inverness," I ventured.

"So you're going to Dornoch, then," said the news butcher, dusting his candy and magazine cart. "Sure and that is one of the world's greatest unnaturally natural courses . . . and most secret, too. You'll be fighting no crowd there."

"It couldn't have been secret long if Old Tom Morris laid it out." At last I was able to lay in a tidy fact myself.

"However, do you know Dornoch now is our truest seaside links?" bustled the conductor. "I ask you, bear with me, sir, and your ladyship, simply consider the fourteenth hole. Foxy is such a grand piece of landscape with fiendish demands. If one hits two stout shots, one fully regards the green; but will the chip shot then remain on that hearth? Memory was awed by recollection of hazards and "sudden death" on the turf. They appeared in accord on this one. Destiny was usually a partner in golf.

"But then Dornoch, too, has no royal designation. Like Carnoustie, it has been a Cinderella." The conductor liked his image. They all did, I could tell. "An abandoned drudge of a waifish links clutching the North Sea strand," said Tickets. "Aye, but she'll be recognized one day. A prince will come for the great awakening." The conductor sighed. L.P. was beguiled by the northern imagery and beckoning legends.

"Well, Carnoustie and Dornoch are unlike, but both are world-esteemed courses. We certainly know them in America. And think of old Donald Ross. My dad thought he was a king." I almost smirked. Another obscure fact to impress L.P., and she was, too. It helps to remember a name or two, and the odd phrase.

"There you see," exclaimed Tickets. "It *was* old Donald who laid out the fourteenth and that heartless green."

"But then," I exclaimed, firing my final bolt, "if we think of Carnoustie and Dornoch as non-royal, what of your great Turnberry?" Not a hair was turned. The train chugged on.

"Aye, well . . . the clubhouse is certainly better, and while Dornoch is the greatest course in the north, it might be that the Strathclyde's great course might be the greatest links down in the west."

"But you hesitate . . . the flying field from World War II was all removed, I thought . . . all covered over, thank God."

They nodded in unison, gravely. Maybe grimly. Surely in all the gross-ness of war the Heinkels could not have destroyed an entire golf course!

"Is the fine clubhouse intact?"

"Oh yes, it served as a club throughout the war. A mess for flying officers. You see, the course was changed . . . yes, 'changed' best describes it. Turnberry is now a huge flying field . . . an aerodrome. There is concrete everywhere for three long landing strips . . . and gun batteries." Tickets clucked and clicked his punch. The shame of it. War *is* hell.

"Oh, oh, oh. I had no idea such a gross thing had happened!"

"Aye, the course has suffered and the land all about it. But then Bruce's castle and all about it bespeak the dogs of war through many a century. When the old Marquis of Ailsa installed the links he was seeking privacy . . . solitude . . . private person golf." The conductor was waxing, and he had all my attention.

Of course this was long before the first thirteen rules of golf were drawn up in 1744 by the Company of Gentlemen Golfers, the Honourable Company, now resident at Muirfield. The Edinburgh Council even provided a silver cup; and the rules, which state that a ball must be played "where it lyes, if stopped by a person, horse, or dog," were transferred in principle to the Royal and Ancient.

Bonny Prince Charlie's surgeon, John Rattray, was captured at Culloden and given the death sentence. The appeal judge was a golfer too and freed his fellow member. Nothing new about "networking!"

"Nonetheless," Tickets offered, "Robert Bruce is long gone from memory, and so are Wallace and the R.A.F. They say MacKenzie Ross and Frank Hole will now lead the charge to former greatness."

"With a name like Hole he's got to be the one," I offered. Only L.P. appeared amused. So I plunged on. "And surely the weather for golf is finer over there." Again I was met with gravitas followed by a surge, as I persevered. Weather is sacred business in Scotland, about every ten minutes.

THE ELEVENTH HOLE

"And what, sir, do you esteem as fine weather for golf at Strathclyde?" I was truly stumped.

"What I remember are some seaside holes in the first round." They were hot on the scent again, like terriers.

"Aye, you remember well! Coming off Blaw-Wearie you went on to number four Woe-be-Tide and then the grand Fin-me-oot and that terrible pit, Tappie Toorie, number six."

"And then you remember how we moved on to number seven, Roon and Ben? There was a bright afternoon sun that day, but the wind had come on, and it was 520 yards against the Irish wind. Then Goat's Fell." They were again entranced.

"Another 440 yards." If the engineer had been with us we would have crashed for certain, but the train plunged on.

"Yes, and then Bruce's Castle, such a terrible par four."

"Do you know that was 460 yards across, something more desperate than your Pebble Beach links? We played down there in 1934. It rained."

"I shared their silence and sense of something fine in the past and something good in the future . . . for them, and for us. Could the grand old course be retrieved? Of course it could, with ardency like this. And much else, besides.

The next morning we had another lucky break on the northern rail line, the time and weather. During the night I had been thinking about the three huge steel girders of the Firth Bridge, wondering why the Germans had not effectively bombed them; but my further thoughts were about the immensity of that wondrous engineering project, begun well over sixty years ago. Many was the train of Highland regiments that had moved south from Inverness on the way to who knows what domain of Victoria's . . . or on which continent. All those bonny regiments, their pipes, drums, standards, and tradition. Regiments are in truth to die for.

I could just make out the majestic rises of Dornoch in the fast-rising sun, but there seemed to be no one about the fine-looking station hotel. Then we passed some homely ruins of the ducal Sutherland families; and some purposeful salmon anglers were moving along the paths and roads behind their ghillies. It is quite a remarkable scene on an unruffled morning. A somewhat bomb-scarred, remote, and unremarkable county town is Dornoch, calmly presenting an utterly splendid beach and a truly magnificent course, as the train crew had essayed the day before. Calm and remote, yes, but utterly drenched in history, much of it dark. I could just make out the clock tower of the clubhouse, just off the trap-encircled eighteenth green.

L.P. and I were involved with other plans far to the north, and despite the attractions, we moved on, knowing that we would somehow return.

Curiously, the long beach I could just glimpse beyond Turnberry reminded me of an early dawn hour on the beach at Waikiki, midway through the Pacific war, when I had played a series of five irons along the deserted shore between the grand old Moana Hotel and the incomparable Halikalani. The sense of golf and sense of time were for a few moments mutually incompatible as the tropic sun vaulted, the ball rose and fell only at my stroke, and the lazy waves moved rhythmically in from the battles far out at sea. I supposed that patient and much-besieged Robert the Bruce would have had some philosophical insight into all of that. There must always be time for the simple pleasures of play, I mused, thinking my sentiment almost an apt quote of good King Edward the Seventh.

THE ELEVENTH HOLE

157

For an entire long day in the railcar my clubs had been taken for granted, but as we left the grand old Inverness Station Hotel early the next morning heading north, some anxious looks were cast at my luggage.

The stalwart and splendid statue of the Crimean Highlander (surely from Colin Campbell's old 93rd of Balaclava fame) stood stoic outside Inverness Station, ramrod straight in wind-etched granite. How many highland lads had he honored, standing forever rigid to see another bonny detachment off to some English or Lowland depot from his sentry post at Inverness station; and to how many forgotten campaigns? What about those Highland regiments? Beyond compare in their performance at the Pyramids, at Alma and Lucknow.

We scrambled aboard the ferry at Wick, which had been holding for the boat train rather than at the lonely naval piers at John O'Groats. By the time we reached the Pentland Firth, darkness had rushed in, and the chop on the racing tide was a serious consideration.

L.P. knit furiously from her wonderful new yarn balls bought from an optimistic woman in a lonely booth beside the pier. I happily counted my golf balls, although with some mounting alarm. There were some Fairways, at least three Tigers and two Hagen Honey Centers, three U.S. Nobby Seniors, and two badly nicked K-28s. Also a Dash, plus a big stash of tees. As the wind whistled through the upper works of the tiny ferry, L.P. reached into her bottomless reticule. An imposing silver flask, which had once belonged to a dissolute English earl, came out to play in the tiny saloon lights. At last, cognac, of whatever description or pedigree. The elixir of life. Everything rapidly fell into place. Order was restored, as was I.

"So now fill me in on these clubs we're doggedly packing around," said L.P., deftly pouring two more fine drams.

We were, by the way, the only passengers aboard the *Peregrine*. My spirits were altogether ignited. So I was able to respond easily and reasonably, at least it seemed so at the time. "Well, you won't believe this. . . . There is some impulse at play here."

"Well, try me . . . again."

"I never believed we would have this permission to go north so late in the season. And besides, Scapa Flow is still filled with every kind of naval ship, German and Italian trophies and a hundred mine fields and net barriers. Besides, they are paying off all kinds of H.M. ships here because of the money crisis; and it probably gets a bit rowdy.

"Anyway, when we were leaving our apartment back home I looked at the scale map for just a second. I spotted a tiny flag marker on the chart just below Stromness, on the edge of Hoy Sound, which looks down a long bank toward the Scapa Anchorage. I knew that it was a golf marker! Nine holes. So I thought, what a spot! Maybe the Ultima Thule in golf links. Anyway, it seemed worth a shot." L.P. blanched; I was too amused with my little word play. Besides, I was talking too much. Cognac tugs the sense of deportment.

"I can see the attraction. In the footsteps, or maybe divots, of great golfing admirals . . . if there were any."

"Something like that, I suppose."

"Well, at least the trees will be tiny, and it is an immense and legendary anchorage. No flowers to smell, either."

"I don't think there are *any* trees. There used to be great forests. But the views should be vast, maybe even sublime. The way I see it we should pound away in the ancient and ill-lit Kirkwall archives for four full days, then move over to Stromness for Friday and Saturday. We can restore some long distance vision to see what might be there, and then on Sunday play an early game before we fly back to Inverness."

"Well, it sounds good to me except for the Sunday bit. Things are apt to be a bit different up here, something like the Outer Hebrides. No golf on Sunday, no fishing, no fires, no nothing. Or had you forgotten John Knox?"

I fell silent. But a new thought struck me. "What if it's a naval course? Think of Earl Jellicoe and his brother-in-law Charles Madden! Do you think those vigorous sea dogs would have foregone their golf on Sunday?" I sounded quite grand. "And what of Tovey and Fraser?" I moved up one whole war. They were monarchists, not democrats, but it would not have seemed the fair way to keep the golf links to themselves.

We'd have to ask Eric Linklater, but it seems likely. Yes, Linklater would know the ins and outs of this puzzle.

Peregrine was finally secured at the dock, and we pounded through the wind and dark to the cozy little rock-bound hotel, a night light waiting to show us safely in. Happily, we had brought plenty of sandwiches from Inverness, so we huddled in the eiderdowns and munched and savored cognac. We crashed as a stormy autumnal night enveloped our new home and us, snugged down in the ageless foam-bound rocks.

It was an eventful week. Almost every person on the island had been commandeered to bring in the critical potato crop known as "tatties." How they worked! We were maybe lucky to escape. Men, women, and children were in the fields, furiously digging. The schools were shut down. The one week of autumn was in full flood. Winter was coming. The crop must be brought in. I was too strongly reminded of Ireland a hundred years earlier. But on to *the* course! Yes, it was there, all right.

While the weather had been thick and demanding all week, no one stopped working. And that included us, in the archives devoted to

Orkneymen who had taken long- and short-term service with Hudson's Bay Company in the late eighteenth century and for several generations thereafter. Those Bay men were cunning masters. They wanted men in Canada who were already broken in to wind, weather, hardship, and heartache. Yes, it was well worth our journey, though the days were shorter and colder and the Kirkwallians somewhat confounded by our intense concentration on happenings so long ago. But they had through their hard times been faithful record keepers, good stewards of the past.

And we were eventually advised, after some telephone talks of a muffled nature interspersed with long worrisome pauses, that "Yes, the golf links just might be opened for one more day of play." And, "Yes, maybe this one last time . . . on Sunday," the woman gasped. "You've come such a long way, an exception is called for."

I realized later, but not much later, that my real drive to get up to the Orkneys was perhaps not so much the archives as the historic outlook, an unbroken vista southwest from the Scapa Flow golf course. From the greens and fairways of all nine holes, golfers through the world's two greatest wars could gaze upon endless parades of British naval might from Lord Fisher and Madden in the *Dreadnought,* on through a wakeful half-century of implacable control. It was all so grand, and so very wrongheaded and pitilessly human in judgments. War is insane; we all know that. Of course we do.

But what a perfect Sunday morning it was for golf! L.P. and I pulled up near the rustic cottage marking the club headquarters and the first tee. Admiral Beatty couldn't have spent much time in such sparse amenities. He might have preferred his fortune teller or Irish hunters. But two things instantly took our eyes. There were over a dozen ruddy, outdoor men of middle years gathered in the brilliant ten o'clock sunlight, including three or four projecting that always curious sense of command. Distant blue eyes, naturally. And down the slope beyond the men, spread out across the glittering anchorage, were the still impressive remnants of what was for two centuries the world's most powerful fleet. But now no more. So many magnificent and mossy traditions, too many unsung heroes. Gallantry can be a curse, a glorious one.

Whatever my thoughts, the squadrons anchored in the broad roadsteads of Scapa Flow were immensely impressive, dramatic in their hulking power. They were lying low and menacing, still in wartime gray and dazzle camouflage; somnolent, but surrounded by coveys of prizes, including row upon row of U-boats surrendered in May and June of '45. I was stunned by the so clearly revealed view, even more than I expected in the blinding light of late fall. The clubhouse clock rang four bells. One can handle just so many distractions.

The men waiting to tee off were far more interested in us. More to the point, I could see that it was my bag of clubs which drew them forward. The reason was quickly apparent. Each ancient canvas or leather bag present contained several wood-shafted clubs with forged heads. Most were familiar, one way or another, but others were of ancient and original designs—hickory shafts and long, hand-forged iron heads. There were bulger drivers, cleeks, and mashies and mid irons galore . . . and pullers of wood. The players soon made it clear that their course was open for play this Sunday only because of L.P. and me. The magnificent exception. And they were grateful. It would close until spring thaw at the end of our game. They were in fact jubilant at the prospect, in a northern, close-held way. Basically, they glowed in semi-silence. One more game. Perhaps an ace!

The imposing player who relayed necessary information in a somewhat laconic yet pleasant manner eventually identified himself as the executive officer of the *Vanguard*, a massive battleship quietly swaying at anchor some distance off.

"She's a great sight, Commander," I ventured. "Her lines look like the last word in marine design."

"Thank you, sir. Yes, *Vanguard* represents all that we learned about naval construction. But she never fired a shot in anger. Those turrets just missed the big action at Normandy. However, if you want to see a truly historic ship, there's *Warspite* just off *Vanguard*'s starboard bow. She may very well be our most illustrious warship. I'd say certainly the very greatest naval legend in this century. From Jutland to Normandy to Japan, ever victorious."

"What about *Hood* or *Barham*?"

"Well, for one thing," he replied evenly, *Warspite* is still afloat. But then, too, there were *Iron Duke* and *Queen Elizabeth*. Denizens."

I also thought about the illustrious *Royal Oak*, now resting on the bottom of the Flow with audacious Prien's German torpedo shots in her from 1939. A cloud of mist was gathering, suddenly sweeping along down across the bare hills and rune stones from the northeast. The temperature was sliding very rapidly as we accepted the compliment of teeing off first. No practice swing. What a drive I had, curving down the long, sloping fairway of coarse grass. Thank heavens I got off the first tee with some dash. The *Vanguard*'s exec and two wiry men from Stromness joined us. L.P. was more interested in the thousands of white birds filling the blue sky above us, keening and careening along a black storm front.

And what a front it was! On the first hole I took a par four. On the second, it took me eight hard strokes simply to punch through to the green against the driving wind. And in truth, my ball would not sit still on the green. Scapa, in fact, is where I first heard about Admiral Beaufort's wind scale, but his nineteenth-century descriptions did not truly apply. In Scapa there is really nothing to be blown away, the commander reported, excepting the warming shack-clubhouse and the players themselves.

On the sixth hole I realized that it was no longer a sporting event. The cruel wind again brought to mind an ancient Hudson's Bay saying from the Canadian Arctic, "a scrotum-shrinking experience." It was just likely the phrase originated here in the Orkneys—a more literate place than the Arctic.

Perhaps when most reflections of the bright men and women of the Orkneys have faded in my vision, metaphysical memories of some trillions of wheeling birds will flash across my screen, wheeling in out of the surf, down out of the sun, scudding across the sere turf of the links. A sight provided by the gods and nature: red-throated and great northern divers, fulmers and Whooper swans, Purple sandpipers and red-breasted mergansers, hen harriers and Twites, kittiwakes and Great skuas and endless wheels of guillemots and Arctic terns.

And of course L.P. identified them all, except for the Short-eared owls swooping over the rocky, chambered tombs of Harray and the standing stones of Stenness; and then a pair of swooping peregrines, diving toward Scapa like preying bombers from Europe. They were my double offering. Then, too, these were the birds of late fall. One could wonder what the summer skies revealed; was there enough air to support all those lyric wings?

But while L.P. made formal bird-sighting notes I was staring intently at some ancient but utterly splendid golf shoes. One of our crowd was hobbling along in the grandest leather ever seen—my caddie, whom I had engaged to avoid his acute distress. Casually I commented once again on the famous figures who must have played the course: Jellicoe, Madden, Tovey, Troubridge, or Max Horton. I was prepared to go on.

"And don't forget the King," chimed in our caddie, "Old George the Fifth, God bless him!"

"Yes, this should be designated a Royal Golf Course. Even the old Duke of Connaught had a birdie on six." And the caddie chimed in again.

"And the Prince of Wales, God bless him, took an eight on the ninth. He was so chagrined he left his golf shoes behind him." He grinned the smirk of one supremely satisfied. I now knew where his shoes had come from. Just so . . . Cork Street. The Prince must have winced when he discovered the loss, not to mention his valet!

What I was yearning for was the stout tartan cap the Prince usually wore on the British links. What a wind it was! My eyes streamed, but this was no time to give in to Zeus.

Somehow we all staggered through to the end and we gathered to share L.P.'s Rémy. In the warming hut we passed around the special golfing flask and our new partners savored the last drops of the inspirational liquor. Then to further honor the singular occasion, two bottles of single malt mysteriously appeared . . . yes, even on Sunday. One of the wiry heroes intoned in the curiously sonorous voices they own that "force eight or no, it was certainly better for aged backs than digging tatties." Staring across the now rime-covered ninth green, the commander allowed that "it also beat a middle watch in December on the Murmansk run." Agreement was general. Memory!

Yes, L.P. and I had come to see a storied piece of military landscape, or rather seascape, and it was all that we could have imagined. The words of Baron von Humboldt came to mind as he peered down into Khyber Pass in

1832: "Locality is the only surviving reality of a historical event that has long ago passed by." A great statement and clearly delineated; and oh, so strategically placed Scapa responded to the Teutonic observation in spades. The fifty-two half-obscured, disarmed Nazi submarines seemed to bob and nod in further agreement.

"Is there anything left of the old German Imperial fleet scuttled by the officers and men in 1919?" Some silence surrounded my question.

"Almost nothing to be seen," an old-timer reflected through clouds of smoke. "But you know there's a wee bit of a story I find appealing. At the time of Dunkirk, when every floatable thing was sent over to save the armies, we also sent down Admiral von Reuter's long-preserved private launch, the *Count Dracula*. Now that, that makes a story." We all howled, along with the wind. "We staked everything." Another great howl of laughter.

And then it was time to go. Some of the men had actually been using Gutta Percha balls, and I thought we should at least leave our Honey Centers behind for next year's play. Off we went through the rune stones and sleet to the so-called airport.

I made some notes in my tiny travel diary while we waited out the inbound Inverness plane. Masses of clouds and sheets of sleet swirled and rattled around the walls of the lair-like waiting room. The flight might well be canceled from Inverness, I reflected. We were out of our critical supplies.

"Did you notice?" said L.P. "You were the only one using wooden tees. They were all making sand tees."

"Yes, but the wind was blowing their tees down before a ball could be hit. Actually, I left all of our tees in the hut for next spring. Let's hope the mice don't eat them."

"That's the only loose wood on the islands, as far as I can see. Tees could be an acquired taste."

INCREDIBLE LIES

"Yes, but all these rocks were once covered with trees like the then clad Hebrides."

Then I queried the station manager about the plane once more. She was standing at the alert, sprightly in her potato digging costume.

"I can just hear it now, sir," she lilted. "He's feeling his way down. Tim says it's like feeling your way down the stairs in the dark."

"He must be using his landing assistance system. At least some radio beacon or radar."

"Oh no, sir. That was all taken away with the Armistice. We only have the basics—beacons and flares and such like."

"Well, there's all kinds of new radar equipment coming along for air fields. When do you think you'll get yours installed?" I nervously polished my clubs, cocking my ears.

"Oh never, sir. You see this really is Ultima Thule. The ends of the earth." She vanished with a twinkle, lugging a huge torch.

And then there was the plane, suddenly pulled close up to the building. The pilot was already turned, ready to scud away home toward Inverness. Mail there was, but two passengers were a dividend.

As our plane worked its way up into the clouds I thought of the second foursome in our group. One fine old gent had eventually identified himself as "Hudson's Bay Company, retired, and All-Arctic Champion from 1920 to 1928." Imagine! Some time we would have to find his course, with tundra fairways no doubt.

But again Scapa was a long ago reverie, at least for the moment it appeared so. On the way down through the sleet to Inverness field I said a prayer for the entombed men of the *Royal Oak*. And one for ourselves.

THE ELEVENTH HOLE

As I sauntered toward Firclad's third tee (also the twelfth), I was struck once again by what had diverted me in the large trap bordering the second green. Nowhere before had I seen molehills, that is, fresh earth mounds pushing up in a regular pattern through sand. Tiny mountains. For some reason the appearance caused me to think once more of our long ago "bold tourney" and its closing hours on the slopes of Mount St. Helens.

. . . .

My perhaps wistful memory was that we had almost bounded up the mountain in our late-youth enthusiasm. After two strenuous hours of hard driving, pushing through the dense valley mist, we had reached a 7,000 foot elevation, just above the heavy fog belt and just below the snow line. A day beyond compare.

A light wind from the west played across the lava and pumice slopes with a general crystalline effect in the blinding unobstructed sunlight. Newtonian charismatic, of course, our game was; but even more was the prismatic quality where hard sun rays caught the billions of snow and pumice crystals tumbling through the cloudless alpine air. But even more memorable now about our unique game in the sky was something we ought to have noted then, at least to noodle among ourselves. Let me describe.

At the end of the first five "rough holes" Gerry had laid out (with substantial loss to his golf balls, shoes, and trousers), we took our ease in a low-lying patch of windbreak huckleberry bushes. What I still remember today was the slight shiver I noticed in the branches and young leaves around us. Just the barest discernible shudder of the ruby bright new leaves, the hundreds of tiny little pumice slides constantly eddying all around us; secret slides, scarcely visible except to the most searching eye. In other words, all during that long ecstatic summer afternoon our much-revered volcanic peak was even then signaling a continuing subterranean life of its own. Dormant it most certainly was not, had we but concentrated a moment on what was happening along our hastily laid-out alpine course. But of course our minds were on the driest of dry martinis we were drinking, the finest of shots we were going to make on the last two holes, and the beautiful ladies joining us for late dinner that long and lazy high summer evening.

Of course, our perfectly beautiful Mount St. Helens would not lose her head, not turn hellion for almost a generation. But even now I recall the subtle, but distinguishable signs of a highly intemperate volcanic cone which blew apart in 1980 along with many storied dreams of childhood: Spirit Lake, wilderness, the cosmos. I simply did not comprehend the smoldering Vulcan furnaces beneath our feet. But again I digress.

· · · ·

Remembering yesterday's Firclad shot into the swarming goldfinches, I now narrowly regarded their grand tree. True birds of passage, they. The massive maple limbs were empty. Drawing out a baffie for a first-time use, I tried out the flat backswing of Scotland, which had returned to my mind that morning. How I loved the memory of that long-ago game.

Should I say, without seeming to try, I again drove two relatively new balls in a set of successive hooks into the towering woods. They entered the dense foliage soundlessly. In golf one really has only one person to take into basic account on a hole-by-hole, shot-by-shot basis. The greatest American game is quite otherwise, with eighteen players to consider. In golf, one plays essentially against or with oneself.

I thought about my scores over the last two days. Unbelievable they were, of course, but the greatest source of disbelief was the continuing erratic quality. In every sense mine was a flawed style, and yet was it? Why not express some amazement at the magical quality of *some* of my shots, and forget the time spent in deep pits, bogs, and dark forests? "Take time to smell the flowers," Hagen said. And I agreed. Very laid back, that philosophy, and made for the private player. Hard, yes, but with grace—Chandler Egan style. In golf as elsewhere it's sensible to seek models.

I was reminded of one other time when I had, for a fleeting hour or two returned to the great game, although this was more of an imperial theme than vague reverie.

· · · ·

More than twenty years before on a spring morning, I had checked out of the grand old Fujiya Hotel near Hakone, south of Tokyo. An impassive driver, elegant in white gloves and dust flick, was waiting to carry me over the Odawara passes to Atami Station, there to continue my journey to the Sea of Japan. The views of Fujiyama cone were magnificent that morning, an unlooked-for treat comparing most favorably in height and form to St. Helens—the reminder. As my car rose out of the forest and breasted the first of five passes, I saw a welcome sight across the picturesque landscape of the Floating World.

There, just below me and running generally down toward the Pacific, was a golf course made in heaven. Of course its altitude was heavenly, but so indeed was every aspect of it, as though from the atelier of the imperial landscaper. Each fairway was hand-groomed. Ordered groups, purposeful players, and female caddies moved sedately across deep-turfed mountain swales as though in a surrealistic dream of that final great golf layout in the sky. I entered a note in my travel diary. A beautiful sequestered course with few players and an elegant sense of time; spacious and unhurried. Some day I would return and I remarked to myself that the course looked as though it would welcome a few more players. A ball sped off toward the Inland Sea. The player seemed relaxed in time and space, unhurried, the Japan of Lafcadio Hearn.

THE ELEVENTH HOLE

THE TWELFTH HOLE

B ut now was the time to move down Firclad's third fairway toward the conclusion of my solitary wandering. The romantic poet as golfer. Actually, that vision is more pleasing than quirky; strong rather than wimpy. And besides, some Japanese might be intrigued by a less-intense approach to the undulating fairways of Nipon; less closely clipped, more Zen than Bushido.

Somewhat soothed by this Far Eastern philosophy, I ambled down the fairway. A cloud of birds burst into song, not a chirruping or twittering sound but rather something melodious, rhapsodic. Birdsong, I suppose one might properly call it. It was remarkable to me because I hadn't thought before about actual songbirds in the Northwest. More in evidence were birds of a more raucous sort. The meadowlark and Redwing black-birds were pleasing exceptions, of course, and the rather melancholy mourning dove. Yes, raucous was the word for crows (always too many), the startling Steller's jay of the blue streak; and even gabbling Canada geese and varied ducks, not to mention the startled cry of a Chinese Ring-necked pheasant or the Hungarian partridge.

Only last week in the club bar in town I had bitten hard when a chap had casually told me he knew the secret of bringing succulent chukars to the dinner table. I naturally responded, "Tell me immediately, do you use a sixteen- or a twenty-gauge gun?" He smirked and said, "You drive fast along the backroads of the high desert at dusk and then simply remove them from the grill of your car and serve." Very funny. I was pained. But it wasn't bad, really. Grilled chukar.

But now I was striding along with my reduced bag over my shoulder recalling the memorable deluge of last night's rain and the invigorating mists of early morning. It was wafting and blowing away in a shimmer across the ranging hills, leaving a sunlit morning of heart-tugging beauty. Sweet, heaven-sent harmony. The richest odors reaching deep down into my childhood eddied from the dense green forest verdure beside me. There was a oneness, a timeless wholeness-with-the-universe sense about it all that I instantly associated with youth. Curiously, this made me think about the amazing number of splendid spotted leopard slugs stretched out, haughtily taking their insolent ease on the matted forest floor. Just possibly my errant balls were lolling on such a winter speckled carpet, damp and loam gray. It had happened before.

. . . .

I suddenly thought of the old number five hole of my youth, where I had been prowling one wet afternoon in the late thirties. Naturally I was looking for balls to sell, building up some dollars to buy my first pair of grown-up cords. The thought of such a meaningful purchase had me down on my knickered knees, scratching through the dense salal. Suddenly into my vision came a fine pair of argyle socks and stout plus fours. Staring down at me with calm brown eyes was a well-known habitué of the club, Roderick Brandon. He coughed lightly as he regarded my small but bulging sack of balls. I remembered he had seen service in the infantry on the edge of the Argonne years earlier. The cough was permanent. "Kid, you seem to be better at this than I am, at least today." I was thunderstruck and stammered a bit, momentarily confused. He looked distant, yet mildly amused. At ease.

"Sir, are you looking for balls too?" It was actually against the unwritten rules. Not done, not even caddies. But members, ye gods, no! We all understood that Mr. Brandon was always broke.

"As a matter of fact I am, especially a new one I drove into this stand of alder last week." He poked vigorously about in the maples. "The truth of it is that I'm out of golf balls and so is my wife. Strange as it may seem to you, neither of us can play in the tournament tomorrow unless I turn up some balls." There it was, plainly said. He ruminated and thrashed about some more. "There's a saying about that some place or other." Chuckling, he pulled back a spreading fir branch and snatched up a ball from the moss. "There it is . . . .

Mr. Brandon seemed to very naturally pass the time of day, blithely breaking the "no-no" rules of the course. "The truth is," said he, picking up another scarred but still usable ball, "there is a full set of ladies' clubs and an almost new men's bag registered as the first prize for best low ball score. And the two of us have an understanding."

He coughed again shallowly, and I realized somehow that I might ask about the understanding. At my age, nothing about any relationship between men and women was beneath notice. So I said it right out.

"What understanding, sir?"

"Well, if we can win the tournament, my wife will finally have good equipment. And there's a rumor going around that the soldiers' bonus may be paid at last. If I get a check, finally I'll be able to buy a whole set of new clubs: First Flights, steel shaft irons, and some Lawson Little woods." He smiled reflectively, or maybe it was dreamily.

It was strange, or let's say odd, to me. Just the other day one of my brothers had asked our dad how come Roderick Brandon could play golf all the time when he was on federal relief. My dad came through with one of his tried and true replies: "It was one of life's mysteries, which are legion." He continued, "And besides, he was a second lieutenant, of no present use to the army or civilian life where there were no jobs for him to worry about anyway."

Something must have gone right, because later that spring I saw them both on the course, the best turned-out couple ever. People said they made their own clothes—that is, she did. And they looked absolutely right. To which my father again remarked, "You can't buy taste, try as you might; and the Brandons have it from head to toe. *Ton* is the word." I made a note of it. A good sound, short and sweet.

A few years later Rod, as I eventually learned to call him, went back into service in charge of all the army golf courses in the continental United States, and Hawaii too. He was reshaping the seventh green in Honolulu when some Japanese Sunday bombs tore up the turf and supplied him with an unplanned sand trap. When I saw him after the war he laughed and said, "I was on the seventh the morning of the seventh, but damn it, they put the new bunker on the wrong side of the green." I saw the bunker recently at the de Russie course. There's even a historical plaque.

• • • •

I was deep into this fifty-year-old reverie as I stepped off the fairway and over a tiny trickle of brook laced with field mouse tracks. Above me a brooding owl hooted, one no doubt sated with tiny mice, voles, and moles. Again my nose was assailed by a very heavy pungent odor, the wind carrying toward me from a dense copse of hazelnut trees. It was much sharper than elk or deer, and certainly not of the skunk family. Nor was it truffles. I rather abstractedly thought of a cougar, as we called them, the well-known mountain lion or panther. A "painter" in the language of Daniel Boone and other woodsmen. Could it be? This close to town, and among so many people? I had seen them long ago, but this was another time and cougars do not eat hazelnuts—delicious as they are, especially in a daiquiri. Even so, I was as usual more curious than careful.

I drew back the heavy cedar branch screening the view and gasped. I inhaled and then gasped aloud again in sheer fright. There was a monstrous shape sitting in a mud hole.

An absolutely huge, ferocious, dark brown, almost black bear was veering toward me, swiftly rising up from the ground. He roared and snarled horribly from his immense mouth and gaping jaws, which were filled with masses of long and golden ivory teeth and a bottomless dark red throat. One of my two out-of-bounds balls was lodged on a razor-sharp incisor, along with a gross of yellow skunk cabbage. He had been engrossed in pulling it up when I surprised him downwind from behind. Bears are twice as deadly when surprised. His fur was hanging loose in mats . . . I was looking at the results of a very late hibernation. A wild bear!

Old, mangy, out of sorts, and HUGE. Not Lucky Pierre's at all. No one had ever suggested such a lurid misadventure. Deadly, especially when immersed in late-blooming *Lysichtium americanum*.

I was almost petrified with fright. It was useless to run. Bears don't like noise. What to do? I shouted. Squeaked is more like it. Then I screamed and finally roared. It was useless. His large yellow eyes rolled around in the back of his head and a long red tongue drooled across the errant golf ball. My ball! Without thinking another second I whipped out my two iron and put it to my shoulder. "Bang! . . . Bang!" I croaked, amazed at my speed and cleverness. My feint made no impression on the frightening hulk. He stood up well above me, blocking what light there was. Such arms. Terrible breath, too.

The beast was obviously shocked, but more obviously enraged, a bad combination. Furthermore, he now had my club in his claws, easily jerking it out of my shaking fingers. Happily I noted that it was not, after all, my two iron he was bending at a ninety-degree angle, but my former four iron, a less-favored club. His snarling was awful. Someone must surely hear his roars besides the chattering squirrels whose skimpy nut reserves he had also pillaged. There was no way to back off, because a bear can even outrun a horse . . . at least for a time.

As he advanced and loomed over me, great razor-clawed paws slashing about, I was suddenly reminded of an old-time southern woodsman in the Marine Corps who had filled me in one day on the peculiar sensitivity of the bruin's "genial regions." My gunnery sergeant had a peculiar way with the phrases. Now "Gunny's" chosen words from the swamps of Okeechobee made sense.

In a trice I pulled out my driver. Employing my legendary backswing of lightning speed and power, I cracked bruin fair in the scrotum. He stopped dead in his tracks and then crashed in an agonized heap on top of my mid iron. A reproachful howl escaped his long jaws, slightly cracked open by my neatly anchored ball. And of course I was still shaking from head to foot. The whole encounter had lasted no more than half a minute, yet I had every reason to believe my hair might have turned white, including both eyebrows. As I retreated through the fully dappled forest, a long bold ray of morning sun reached down to flood over my second ball, nestled on a bed of rich moss and lichens. "A ball in the hand," said I, "is worth two in the brush." Within a second it was pocketed.

Now who would believe this bear story? No one. How I had driven two balls into the forest, well, four actually, one of which was snatched by a hungry bear. How I had then struck two balls simultaneously . . . and yet had time to retrieve still another ball! Roderick, I think, would be very pleased with me, gazing down from one of the broad fairways of heaven. And maybe Lawson Little, too, or Sammy the Slammer. He knew some special West Virginia bear stories. But there was only one person who would believe without question. L.P., my life partner, would fully understand my horrifying encounter because of other episodes; but I would have to make it very good indeed. Stories must be presented; told well, with aplomb, with style and some sense of affection. And yes, with *ton*. I played out the rest of the hole without incident, but still, despite my true-life adventure, I had to enter a double bogie; and yes, you may quote me, "I could hardly bear it."

Also, I should note that as I left the thicket I also spied a very red and fresh shred of rabbit skin fluffed out in the breeze, swaying from a very long and thorny blackberry vine. That would account for the plummeting Marsh hawk I had seen in wild gyration as I walked down from the tee. So one of us was not quite so lucky in nature's hour-to-hour crapshoot.

THE THIRTEENTH HOLE

I sat on the fourth tee (the scored "thirteenth") and recovered myself. As in Chekhov's wild *The Marriage Proposal*, I continued to experience "some kind of palpitations." Even so, I wondered that I was not more seriously affected. After all, the bear had scared the living hell out of me. And there was my scarred club to prove the ferocity of that moment. But then I remembered an incident of long ago which just might have tempered my alarm, or more realistically my terror and fright. One does acquire, one way or another, a sense of proportion; usually after the fact. Bears can't see worth a damn, being very short-sighted. But their claws are very long and sharpened every day, as any weary forester will attest. Was delayed shock getting the better of me? And who would believe another story?

. . . .

But no, I was actually thinking several years back, 1968, I think, when the grand and demanding course had opened at Puerto Vallarta—eighteen very long and well laid-out tropical holes up the Mexican coast. L.P. had remained down in the town, swimming endless laps in the broad pool beside the *playa*; but of course I just had to see my first Mexican golf course. Shipping golf clubs around the country has never appealed to me, especially on international flights. Nonetheless, I did arrive in Puerto Vallarta with my favorite putter, boasting a hickory shaft and cold-rolled iron head from Prestwick. I had a sentimental attachment to it because of several phenomenal clutch putts I had sunk as an undependable, sometimes brilliant boy wonder.

Much to my dismay, when the hair-raising taxi driver left me alone at the imposing new clubhouse and drove off to park his heap in the shade, I was trapped. A man and wife from Dallas were waiting to tee off, and the manager who lent me his own clubs insisted, nay directed, that I play with them. "They are not unfamiliar with the course," said he. So much for my *persona privata* experience. I was younger then, and less experienced in the direct response "No" or something feigned, such as "waiting for my foursome" and so forth.

At any rate the Texan was a great strapping fellow, and he hit a mean ball. And his partner was full of spirit with a great swing and an even better figure. Also a cute hat. Unfortunately for Tess, she was wearing far too few clothes for the hot coastal wind and sun, and she seemed slowly to melt away before my eyes. But "Tessie"(as he said) had real grit. I had expected her to retreat into the deep shadows of the clubhouse from the ninth green; but no, Tess carried right through to the second nine holes. I think she was secretly pleased to see her big macho husband being somewhat relentlessly put in a defensive mode by a person who does not like to be deprived of his privacy. Aside from all that, I enjoyed the pickup game and his marvelous strength. He just might have made the tour cut on brute force points.

On the seventeenth hole I hit a superb drive with a slight hook into the rough grass along the dark and fetid, rather baleful-looking bayou. I still have dreams about it, even today. A burst of onshore wind dropped my Titleist in what appeared to be the rough, but offering a nice recovery shot to the green. My Texan tiger followed with a heavy lash from his weighted driver. The ball sailed well past mine where it then struck a palmetto log and dribbled into a stand of lilies and broadleaf plants half in and half out of the black swamp water. "Tessie" and Rocky went ahead in their cart, but then they got caught up looking for my ball, all Southern grace and charm.

After all, they didn't have my kind of caddie's know-how following the flight of a shot and marking very specifically the eventual location. They were a good twenty-five yards from my Titleist's lodging place. Without a practice swing, I quickly shot toward the approximate location of the green and then moved ahead to Rocky's ball. Tess had pretty much caved in by then, but the profusion of exotic petals had brought her to life and she was exclaiming that "there just weren't any blossoms that size in Dallas." Quite an admission, I thought. And as usual, they were at least twenty feet away from the bushy green growth concealing his ball. Naturally I had water snakes on my mind, so I pulled out my trusty golf stick to fend off any reptiles, large or small, harmless or otherwise.

Of course my mind was dwelling on the hundreds of balls my long-necked club had retrieved from all the verdure of North America. Tess would see how neatly it was done, now sitting daintily in the canvassed shade of her cart. I would handle it with humor and grace, but also a two-stroke penalty for Rocky. Ha ha.

Thrash, thrash, thrash! No ball. Then in one horrifying second a scaly saurian monster seemed to explode from the sodden jungle under my feet. A huge, snarling, yellow-bellied, rearing crocodile, with wicked reptilian gold eyes and what seemed like 900 teeth. Long ones. Guinness record size. He was after my right arm, of course, one that had already suffered such

THE THIRTEENTH HOLE

heavy damage through the years. My God, I was so lucky! His enthusiasm or ravenous appetite caused him to miss my putter, which I reflexively punched far down his throat. Crunch went all of his occlusive teeth reflexively. Snap went my hallowed hickory shaft. Crash went the beast, back into the bubbling and now most evil Slough of Despond.

Tess was screaming. She saw it, all right. Rocky was gaping and very white. We didn't finish the hole. We all rode the cart to the clubhouse, where the incredulous manager clucked over our story.

"You should not ride three on a car," said he . . . "and besides, Señor, it was an alligator." I told him that he should make notes, because someday a record-sized croc would be extracted from his innocent swamp. Among other things they would find in his belly would be thirty-two inches of hickory and a Scottish, iron-forged putter, hand stamped "1894." I do wish that she had swallowed my nine iron. Tess said "he," but Rocky and I said her eyes said "she."

Yes, the bear was frightening, but somehow or other in North America we all like to think that we get along with bears, in a manner of speaking; but no one I know has ever had a relationship, symbiotic or otherwise, with a thirty-foot "crocodile"— well, eighteen anyway. The bear surprised and frightened me, yes; but the beast from one fathom had ambushed the solitary walker and simply scared me out of my wits. Furthermore, "she" carried off a famous family trophy, a putter that my father had employed on many occasions. "Smack" it would go across a youthful backside as he patiently murmured once again, "Spare the rod and spoil the child." No one escaped his hickory-inflicted justice.

When I got back into Puerto Vallarta, L.P. was just emerging from the pool, having swum some hundreds of laps, I'm sure. She was puzzled. It appeared I had been drinking, she said, a *lot*. I showed her the leather-wrapped handle, the remains of my putter, now of famous memory. My very patient Life Partner has weathered my many misadventures. She was almost incredulous, but neither did she return to the water that day.

· · · ·

I lolled on Firclad's commodious alder bench in the sun, again reminded of events recollected in tranquillity. Wordsworth and Proust were not golfers, but they were great walkers, something akin to Tommy Armour. I shared their sense of remembrances of things past. In fact, the lucent green of the sword ferns marching along the left fairway reminded me of the exotic artifact always in my bag. I rifled around and pulled out the short, snapped-off putter handle still wrapped with a goatskin grip. Thirty-five years, thirty-six? How long had it been since Elizabeth and errant Richard had brought romance of a sort and the entire load of commercial tourism to the once-lovely beach at Puerto Vallarta? Breaking, as Wordsworth said two centuries ago, "the dreary intercourse of daily life." Certainly in P.V., anyway.

Returning my good luck charm to the bag, I pored over my odd scorecard. What did those vagaries reveal? Such an erratic "round," and yet one might interpret in the melange of twos and nines joyous moments rather than grim and trudging determination, and sweet silent thoughts of strokes and fairways past. Not so much the brilliant mornings, perhaps, as longshadowed afternoons. The essence may be late September, when it seems nothing but the ball moves in the golden sunlight.

THE THIRTEENTH HOLE

· · · ·

Daniel was playing in such an afternoon when he carded eight pars and an ace. It was a great thrill, especially since his ball landed in the cup on the fly, knocking a big chunk out of the bottom of the cup. It was so long ago, he recorded it as a spade mashie shot, a six iron.

To add to the sweet taste, he was pitted against a grim, humorless player. Of him it had been said that he played every match as though it would be his last. Furthermore, he played in a heads-down, withdrawn mode, every molecule in his hard body bent on winning . . . above all else. He even wanted to call "Number 5" when the cup was irretrievably damaged by Daniel's white ball slashing down meteor-like through the sun. Among gentlemen a little banter is understood; the Master and his elegant peers considered a little chaff part of a memorable outing—an essential part of the perfect game.

· · · ·

Looking off toward the southwest, over the ranges of still-uncut firs and cedars, I was reminded of a long-ago English journey to evocative Chartwell. There we tramped over the magnificent grounds of Winston Churchill's garden exile in Kent. My muse then effortlessly led me in a leisurely review of some classic English golf clubs.

I had organized myself to play the very sporting nine at Royal Warlington and then the spare and unrelenting greens and fairways of windblown Sandwich. Because of my eternal regard for "Old Nosey," my game plan included a move with our new son-in-law from Sandwich Bay across to Deal, where "the Iron Duke" had slipped off in 1851. One way or another I had never considered the great field marshal as a golfer, but Wellington would have responded to the deep bunkers and well-protected greens of the Royal Cinque Ports course at Deal. Almost a military operation in itself. For one reason or another I regard the much-touted sixteenth hole as overrated. At least *I* favor the ninth, perhaps because of my birdie there in a sharp wind off the Channel. The Duke's kind of luck I had that day. Yes, fortunately for the nineteenth century he was a lucky general. My continuing reverie was suddenly shattered by motor noises coming from "the bear hole."

• • • •

"I say there, old man, do you mind if we play through? Although there are three of us, you seem to be marching to a slower drumbeat. Or are you playing today?"

It was almost too much. I blinked from my sunny reverie back into the Firclad scene. "Oh no, not all. Forge ahead. By all means." So maybe I was dreaming old dreams once more.

I was momentarily off-stride with three older men and two carts so suddenly on my tee. How they got there unawares I couldn't say; and all rather well turned out. Almost too well, I thought. The latest in windbreakers, in shoes certainly, and their trousers and polo shirts were curiously correct. Too right! But as they warmed up I perceived no natural swing among the three.

Odd as it is, one can pretty well tell who has started to play at six, at thirty-six, or—God help us all—at sixty-six. Doctors should be suspended from practice who send their panther patients out to the course to relax and learn golf in their sixties. More than one kind of stroke was predictable. But the chap here in his mid-sixties certainly was by far the best. *Panache* covered it in one word.

"Kind of you to let us through, sir," said the latest entry, wincing a bit over his labored, by-the-book backswing. What would Beldon say! Despite all the smoothed-out and hammered action at the joints of his swing, it was at best a tortured thing. About $12,000 worth of lessons and professional advice tied up there. However, he seemed to be enjoying it all—and share the wealth, I say. One should never entirely knock the trickle-down theory. But then, too, he was teeing off last, appropriately.

The youngest by far of the three checked his card and noted the dying wind, a breeze beneath Beaufort's notice. "Is this your regular course?" he queried in a tone courteous yet condescending. Very "State Department," or something deep in the Beltline. Deep, deep, almost submerged.

"Well, yes. I'm a member here . . . of short standing, you might say." Why go into detail with a ship passing in the night?

"May I ask your thoughts about this hole? It seems tricky, somehow." It's odd how far the inept can look down their noses.

"Well, that's a good estimate of it, all right. I did well on it yesterday, but it's unpredictable; especially the wind factor."

"There isn't any wind." His gaze into space was lofty.

"I know." I seriously despise condescension, and I sensed that Junior was preparing a putdown of Firclad, my newfound obsession. "Yesterday was yesterday, and today is today."

There was no earthly way to tell them about the double blooming dogwood, the millions of wild canaries or goldfinches, the busy evening grosbeaks, the sudden swirls of varied hummingbirds . . . and certainly not about the unseasonal romps of Lucky Pierre's! How to describe the birds billowing and gusting above the bigleaf maple where my Titleist cracked against the trunk? Or was it my Kro-Flite? That was personal, to be savored in moments of tranquillity. Besides, the birds appeared to have gone north. If I stated that my second shot here yesterday had been a chip into the hopper of a greens mower, no clarifying purpose would be served. So I simply remarked that we all tried to hug the right-hand side of the fairway unless we were feeling a sudden power surge. Curiously, the foxglove had burst into bloom in the warm morning sun.

I could see the ears of the youngest one prick up at that. He was pressing too hard to make a world-class shot.

"How about a straight drive to the green?"

"No reason why not, but I should warn you the green is a mass of triple rolls, and trapped all around."

No one could have been more informative. And no one could have struck a fairer drive. A six-thousand-dollar swing and the ball flying straight and true to plop—to the left, on the upper hillside far into the salal—deep. A second drive followed the first, deeper into the salal and the surrounding stumps of mystery. Well-bred silence reigned.

"It's a good thing I bought plenty of balls," stated $6K matter-of-factly. "But I'll lay one down out there, unless one of mine has rolled down through the rough." What a dreamer! "And now I see; the wind is out there, not here."

The second player removed his dark glasses for the shot. He was lithe and athletic, in a beautifully understated way, with superb but not bulging musculature. I decided he was probably Chinese from the north, or Korean; probably not Japanese or in any way from Indonesia.

My mind suddenly linked on to the magnificent new thirteenth hole across the Blue Canyon at Maikaw in Thailand. A glorious par four. But he had other thoughts . . . far to the north.

THE THIRTEENTH HOLE

"Somehow this reminds me of a favorite third hole on my home course at Kobe, Hirono; but perhaps more so of the sixteenth," said he, casually. "The Kasumigaseki course."

Definitely Japanese, I thought, remembering the stunning Kaname Saruyu course just above Atami Springs. Some day, I conjectured, that course would be played. I would bring it to its knees. So much for diffidence.

"It's a good thing I, too, picked up another packet of balls, Bert, although I have no intention of emulating your example." His ball sliced slightly to the right and struck my maple tree, bouncing smartly back onto the fairway.

"What a perfect shot!" I exclaimed.

"My dear fellow," came his murmured reply; best Oxbridge English, with an oh-so-slight Scottish burr, "there is only one perfect shot. The ace."

I fell silent.

"Besides, I failed to think about the sea wind overhead. The Master would call my shot simply good luck."

Who was this paragon? An accurate quote from the Master! Needless to say, I was speechless. Quoting Robert Tyre Jones, he could do little wrong in my eyes, on the course or off.

The $12K swinger then placed his ball also well along to the right, but nicely positioned for a chip to the green. Pleased with the outcome, he turned to me as the senior player and said, "Why don't you trail along with us? We'd love to have your insights into the course as we evaluate it." They nodded in unison, relieving me of any otiose emotions.

More to the point, I could hardly fail to respond in the fact of such an ominous announcement. "Evaluation?" Whatever did they mean? I quickly teed up and slammed my ball as close to $12K as skill allowed. No practice swing, either.

I was also carried deep into my thoughts by the Japanese address to the ball. Was it the stance, that slight hunch but erect trunk with the power wrists of Ben Hogan? No, it was something quite different, neither English nor American, and certainly not from the rambling links of Scotland.

By George, I exclaimed to myself, it's his grip! It's all in the grip! There was only one swing like that known to me, so carefully and gracefully holding the club like a magician's wand. Let's call it a very special North Atlantic swing, one that belonged to only one ennobled champion: Walter Hagen.

I thought over endless possibilities, my mind in a whirl, as I trailed along behind $12K's cart. He was heading toward the rough, a kind of sedge running beneath a heroic stand of trees, a perfect native group with superb shore pines standing in the foreground, the elegant *Pinus contorta*. And rising up behind was a grouping of Western and Mountain hemlocks supporting these *latifolias* and *heterophyllas*; and with them, in an eight-foot shaggy circumference, stood an "Oregon pine," the *Pseudotsuga menziesii* which we more commonly call a Douglas fir. Hail Scotland! Half obscured in its vast shadow in a mass of sword fern and evergreen huckleberry stood Mac. His mother Tarquil (I'm certain she was so named) would have been speechless at his obvious skulking. And on his own property, too.

He motioned in a vigorous half-second flurry of plowman's hands. The sibilants reached me. "Vip . . . find out what they're doing here." He sank back down in a mass of salmonberry and thimbleberry bushes, *spectabilis* and *parviflorus* of the *rubus* group. What an assignment! Call in Mr. Moto . . . but I could see every reason for his wild curiosity. Who were these men, and why were they at Firclad?

Mr. $6K had laid a ball down on the opposite edge of the narrow, now obviously much too narrow, fairway. I would hate to tell him he was now lying five on this hole, counting his pair of two-stroke penalties. I would have been nonplused, but he wasn't. A brisk chop placed his ball in a beautiful position just beyond the bamboo shaft of the flag: thirty-three inches. I turned back toward Mac, who rose a moment and grinned craftily. He had reset the cup early that morning. "Local knowledge," I mused.

Mr. $12K and I were nestled together, and I showed him the way to the low side of the pin with a lucky chip shot. He followed nervelessly, again placing his ball just inside mine. Did I hear him crow, or was it a sigh of true content? Since he was then almost purring with pleasure, I tried out a question while our fourth player addressed his ball.

I don't think I've seen you around these parts before. Are you with the paper company?"

"Oh no, no. My partner and I are from Washington . . . D.C., that is . . . a quite different center of paper production." He snorted and laughed, cackled actually. I had not expected banter.

Our Japanese fourth then chipped to the rough edge of the green, where his ball hopped and then settled down on a slow purposeful roll to the cup. Almost into the hole. Certainly a gimme.

"Wow," I murmured.

"Actually, I'm sure he is saying the same thing. Probably in Japanese. We have played seventeen courses in the last two weeks—eleven days, actually—and it looks like this might be Mark's first birdie."

"Let's hope so. We'll mark it in your scorecard," said I foxily. "This is a very tough birdie. May you both prevail."

He looked owlish. "Actually, Mark is *our* inside play on words. Our friend says very little other than an occasional mutter about golf, in a curious Tweedy accent. He's from a very old and distinguished family, which is really why we are with him. Practically paid escorts; more like acolytes . . . or train bearers."

"Oh, I see," was my response, though not seeing at all.

"It's a matter of protocol." The $12K birdie prospect was really warming up. "He's actually a marquis in his own right, in the old imperial hierarchy. That is, he will be very soon. Right now he's a baron, but he finds Mark a more convenient name on our travels." He eyed his ball warily. "His great grandfather was the most famous samurai swordsman between Nagasaki and Kushimoto. There is a famous sixteenth-century motto from the Iberian peninsula which he seemed to have adopted for himself from his early Jesuit schooling: *a la espada y el compas / mas y mas y mas y mas.* He successfully fought eighteen hand-to-hand engagements."

"Why eighteen exactly?"

"Simply stated, he lost the nineteenth—plus everything else except the estates and honor. His son inherited . . . Mark's grandfather . . . a disciple of the industrial West."

In the field of information it's always feast or famine. He pulled out his putter and gave me a searching glance. Now it happens I knew and have savored this particular audacious sentiment for years. "Yes, as I recall it, 'to the compass and the sword, more and more and more and more.'" Sometimes there is drama in repetition.

"Yes, very good, with accent on the sword. . . . But not to worry, while Mark is proud of the family motto, he has never practiced the philosophy. Curiously enough, he follows a fairly rough-and-ready philosophy he was taught in the preparatory school in Nagasaki. The Jesuits there operated their school program in the war years, right through to the end. . . ."

THE THIRTEENTH HOLE

He ruminated a moment. "Mark's idea is more toward the idea of the compass; just enough, no less, and maybe just a tiny bit more. He calls it focus."

I turned again to observe this paragon, and with a deeper regard. He was intently studying his score card, while $6ĸ was waiting with some expectation of someone giving him his putt. A vain hope. It wasn't my place to do so; which was too bad, in a way, because the simple-looking putt proved otherwise, thanks to Mac. Rolling well past the cup, it levied two more strokes on the return. I believe he posted a nine on his card. Until then, I gathered, Bert had been well in the lead as medalist. I sighed as Mark sank his putt for a three, successfully followed by $12ĸ. I missed. In a token bit of placatory chatter, I stated that Bobby Jones said, "Golf is the one game I know which becomes more and more difficult the longer one plays it." Mark's eyes glittered in appreciation.

"I can attest to that!" growled $6ĸ, blackening in his card with his very own impossible nine. "What a disaster!"

Mark looked most amiable. "Of course, and I use the word carefully, Robert Jones *is* our master. Dare I say there was no one like him before his time, and no one since? At least not yet."

To say I was charmed hardly describes my curious elation. He was moved to continue. "My father loved to read American history. He said it was so brief he could manage it better than our own rather internecine millennia."

"And did he have some favorite era?"

"Actually, yes. The history of western expansion intrigued him, because your country and all of North America is so vast compared to our tiny islands. Andrew Jackson was a special interest. Especially his British sentiments."

Our game was slowing down considerably in the face of this sudden avalanche of information.

"His second great interest was the history of sports. During his professional career his two obsessions were naval construction and American sports figures."

"Really? How extraordinary," said $12.000 rising suddenly from the green apron to climb into his cart. "Like who?"

"Well, the household staff and certainly my mother knew that the way to distract father from brooding over endless government intrigues, military infighting, and his towering genealogical tree was to mention Babe Ruth or 'Red' Grange, Jack Dempsey or Bill Tilden or Prisk Paddock, the 'fastest man in the world'. Then, too, Walter Hagen and Gene Sarazen, and may I add, Helene Madeson."

"There are some very great names there, all right," said $12K.

"Would you believe that he would sometimes stand in his ancient bonsai garden of maples and pines in the evening and say, 'One must take time to smell the flowers?'" Mark laughed uproariously. "Rhododendrons were his only flowers. All *giganticas*."

We three stared incredulously. A veritable avalanche of good-humored recollections. And a Walter Hagen classic thrown in.

"But his greatest hero was also a Southerner, whom he actually called Son of Old Hickory. That, of course, was your Bobby Jones. My father thought of himself as a kind of Southerner."

"Because he used hickory shafts until the day he retired," said I, going along for the ride.

"Precisely," said Mark, "and at twenty-eight. Truly a laudable age. There my father parted company with Mr. Jones, I'm afraid."

We all fell silent, reflecting on the feats of the Master.

"Well, to round out this unlikely reminiscence, the second big war came. My father simply disappeared from his home and garden one day. Following tradition, I was instantly packed off to military training. Eventually, I was accepted as a naval air cadet. This instantly convinced me that we must be losing the war.

"But I remember on the eve of Father's final departure we were gathered in our family hillside retreat above Kyoto. He took me out into the garden with our golf bags. My two older brothers were already away in the war, and I asked him why he must go again. 'This is my life,' he said, 'and although it's impossible and I dislike it, this is the one that I must play.' In the garden, he very carefully reviewed the Hagen grip with me. You see, Walter Hagen had personally imparted the secret to him sometime in the twenties, during some special British tournament play which Pater had the honor to attend."

We all fell silent again, gazing back across the green with its bamboo shaft and fluttering yellow flag. What a very long time ago, and perhaps a very different age, though no less complex.

THE FOURTEENTH HOLE AGAIN

In this relaxed mood I indicated that the two birdie players should shoot first, which they did with brisk élan. I followed suit, but $6K did not. In a brave attempt to recover, he compressed his swing and duplicated my infamous speed swing, impossible though this might seem. His ball rolled down in the watery sedge, suddenly reminding me of my crash finale at Yale. But he recovered neatly with a second drive seated securely on the apron above the hole. I had not done that.

"Beautiful recovery, Edward," said Mark.

And it most certainly was. An uncommon shot. Much relieved, Edward took his cart to join $12K's, and Mark strolled along with me. We took our ease.

"I have to think there might be something magical about this golf course. I haven't talked this much in years. Especially about myself."

"I agree with you, Mark. There's a bit of magic here. By the way, my name is Tom."

"Really! That was my oldest brother's name—that is, his English name. He enjoyed its solid and simple tone. Like Mark." He chuckled.

"Such a place. 'Far from the madding crowd.'"

"Indeed." I wondered what he would think of Lucky Pierre's and his live-ins, not to mention my quite remarkable bear story. Too early for that. I eyed his outfit once more, and those shoes were from Cork Street, no doubt about it.

"Yes, it's a very quiet place. But I must tell you that I just found this course yesterday." Good heavens, was that only twenty-four hours ago? Life, so unpredictable, so much pleasure and sorrow. Mark moved toward the afternoon shadows, as $12K arrived in his cart. He was unwinding a bit. "Well, Mark ought to play well. His family holds one of the oldest golfing traditions in the Far East."

"How so?"

"Well, maybe he'll tell you one day, but it goes back to 1900, just before the Russo-Japanese War. Are you familiar with that suicidal episode?"

"Oh yes. That's a fracas familiar to us here on the West Coast. Crossing the "t" and all of that. Very bad timing for the Russians, I'd say."

"That's right. Some Scottish engineers, probably from the Clyde River bank, had gone out to the Orient to work up some Japanese yards for naval construction. Mark's grandfather was involved in all those plans."

"And?"

"Along with their endless blueprints and spanners, the Scots naturally brought their bags of clubs and the urge to lay out some golf fairways."

"I suppose that accounts for those early courses around Nagoya and Kobe. They're pretty well established."

"Could be, but from what I've heard the outbreak of the Russo-Japanese War soon attracted some British naval officers. The senior service observers were all crawling through the Japanese woodwork, and a lot of them were long-time golf addicts; the rolling fairways, the tidal swell of the greens, and all that." He chuckled.

"Well, there was some instant rapport, it seems. Deep indicators of the innate good sense of leading families, the landed class, some mutual cachet. The Japanese much admired the British naval traditions, you know . . . and maybe that island sense engenders some sense of mutuality. They also adopted the titles of nobility—baron, count, prince, etc.—along with some imperial fantasies."

"Hadn't thought about that."

"Then too, Mark's family had often been sent up to fight in the north in earlier times. He told me it was the curious equivalent of a Scottish insurrection putting down the hairy Ainus without the colorful legacy of the kilt. A true frontier." He laughed out loud.

"Anyway, after the great naval disasters, the Russians accepted a negotiated peace at Portsmouth, New Hampshire. That was one of the more useful political negotiations in that state . . . world class, in fact, perhaps for the last time."

"I know Teddy Roosevelt thought so."

"Well, after all that whoop-de-do, the Baron was invited back to Britain . . . the other half of the earth's ruling class, and all that. Then later his son went back for training."

"I see. Well, 1905 was a very long time ago."

"I'd say other than arithmetically, a very, very long time ago. Neolithic, in fact. But the curious sense of pride remains the same."

"I couldn't agree more, although I would exclude the word 'curious.' Pride seems pretty much a problem the world over."

"Well, you're right. A curiously stiff-necked kind is. Perhaps an island outlook, especially for those who must always consider a large continental mass nearby; China or Russia, for instance . . . or France and her new partners."

THE FOURTEENTH HOLE AGAIN

"Yes, and I suppose that would include Puerto Rico and Cuba. But in the meantime, I have a difficult approach shot to think through." So much for my very private person statements about golfing. I had almost started talking about myself, which is hardly very private.

But what an opportunity for me to get a bit more insight into golf three or four generations ago! It was hard to keep in focus, really. William IV (our Prince William Henry of northern Pacific geodetic fame) was not only the "sailor king," but, as well, a determined, if not altogether skillful, golfer. But then, too, earlier, so was Charles II's brother, James, the Duke of York. It would seem that this sharer of naval tradition, although a Stuart rather than a Hanoverian, had picked up the so-called Scottish disease when conducting negotiations at Berwick. And of course he was from a Scottish tree, quite unlike the brother of George III. Yes, some of this had to account for the naval passion for golf. Even Beatty had beaten up on the greens of Ireland and Scotland. He probably muttered, "Something appears to be wrong with these clubs today."

I sized up a perfect shot and then fanned the ball . . . I mean grossly . . . while no one was looking. Well, maybe Mac saw it, but it mattered not. Mark seemed to be glowing with inner pleasure and unfeigned surprise. He seemed to be on a roll of good luck.

"I much admire your swing, sir. It seems so natural and well positioned." A lot of basic charm there.

"Well, I actually don't think much about it. If I do, all hell breaks loose."

"Yes, I understand. My father played one day with the Prince of Wales and his younger brother George, the Duke of York. He reported that the senior prince's swing was so flat that it was down around his chest and arms. His brother's was much more lithe and firm, but clear up around his neck; more American than Scottish. Frankly, more graceful. Very reminiscent of Chandler Egan in both form and attire. Especially the fedora. When the Duke of York became king-emperor he seemed to lose some of his form, such as it was."

For the first time Mark bowed slightly, a bit of deference I thought for badmouthing the Emperor of India of long ago.

These matters always hold their own fascination, and I would have listened to more. Mark looked pensively at his lie and then at $6K, who was lost in even deeper thought. Could it be they were playing over their heads? We all were. It's part of the sport. I was reminded again of the course at Deal. I was handily beating our brand new son-in-law relation when the wind changed (just as the Master had warned) and I lost six consecutive holes. A very raw deal!

But now we seemed to hole out with little effort. I thought over our scores: one triple bogie, my par, and two birdies made by two men of upper middle age. They had already puffed up like grouse. "You've brought us luck, sir, I must confess," exclaimed $12K. "These are the times that try us. My first birdie, and no camera available."

Without fuss I drew my small but dependable Chinon Pocket Zoom and snapped several quick candid shots to answer the demands of immortality. A few ounces of camera can make all the difference.

The gentleman from Japan exuded a combination of serenity and inner pride. "These are the moments that release one from the dreary intercourse of daily life," he opined.

"Wordsworth, 1809."

"Yes. It was one of my father's favorite lines. He enjoyed the Lake Country, but what he missed most were the tiny golf links along the Cumbrian coast. Pater enjoyed all aspects of British golf. When he returned home from one famous trip to the United Kingdom, he mentioned playing golf with the Prince of Wales at Sunningdale. When he told us about the Prince on the fifth hole in 1926, our old nannie nearly flew out of her tree. It was a well-known golf calamity."

"You had a nannie . . . in Kyoto?"

"Yes, and our Maudie loved golf! She knew the game from the inside out." I was genuinely amazed.

"Your Bobby Jones had played a perfect sixty-six that summer, with thirty-three putts. Three days later the Prince had lashed three balls in the pond on the famous fifth."

I winced. Bad vibes and associations.

"Nonetheless, Pater managed to lose . . . just narrowly. His revenge came years later . . . Nannie was so relieved to hear that. She said Kyoto reminded her of Carlisle."

I was stunned. Fat chance. "So she belonged to the Scottish borderers then . . . but wherever did your parents find her?"

"Yes, Maudie had come from the border country, but in unlikely fashion, she came to us from Russia. As revolution broke out, she moved across Russia from St. Petersburg by various rail connections with the remnants of her noble family charges; I think with the support of some out-of-favor prince. A cruel and heartless affair it was, all along the Trans-Siberian rail line, but somehow she persevered."

"So she made it all the way to Vladivostok? That's over 6,000 miles!"

"My father said she was his spoils of war from our intervention at Vladivostok in 1918-19. 'A great treasure: knowledge beyond all price,' he reported to Mama upon his triumphant return home. We went to school to her the very next day and never stopped."

He grinned broadly, which the Japanese sometimes do very well, and so sincerely, when amused. An infrequent state.

"Such a great bag of bones she was, but Miss Maudie provided us four crucial things: how to compute, everything about English literature, a great sense of proportion about life—and the etiquette of golf. At least I think so, and so did my father. But I digress." We waited intently.

"After the Great War he was ordered on a long assignment in Britain. When the daily sun swung farther north he would move out of London to the Scottish golf courses. He met Maudie's father there, a long-revered greenskeeper. In the twenties, I think he played them all at least once."

"All?" said I, tentatively.

"Yes. You see, he was following a regime using my grandfather's daily diary showing his early days as one of our country's first golfers. Just so. Using that, my father marked a triangle from Berwick to Troon at Strathclyde with the apex at a most astounding little course in the north. He sent us some wonderful letters home from his visits there in the early thirties, Scapa Flow . . . the great fleet anchorage. The officers had laid out a nine-hole course to circumvent madness."

I gasped, incapable of speech.

"Do you know it? I mean the links, of course," he queried, not a little puzzled.

"Yes, I do by chance. I do."

"Pater said it was a special treat to play with the English bulldogs, the British tars on their great courses. Such insights it provided, views into character and perseverance. And he admired the Senior Service so . . . as do I."

Needless to say, I was much taken with this line of conversation. But an obvious problem loomed. They would be moving on to the top five, which

I had already played. Furthermore, I had a firm date on the river with L.P., who knew nothing about my new acquaintances and possibly a new rare friend. On the green ahead of us I could see Brawn and friends lining up their final putts. Brawn was on the apron practicing, swinging in broad arcs for his next drive. His swing looked strangely familiar. Where had they come from? Were they playing the course backwards? Then I saw Juanita. She had carried out something for them to eat. Big slab sandwiches. Just like the good old days. They had taken their ease in the increasingly bright and warm sunlight. Spacious lollygagging.

"I love this balmy air," said Mark. "There is a small hillside course like this near Kushimoto. It tumbles along the hillsides through stands of black pine and green orange groves above the blue sea. Very striking."

I nodded appreciatively. A pleasing picture. One that I knew, the most southern reach of Honshu. The typhoon center.

"My grandfather was a charter member there before he went to the imperial household. I don't think he ever played again, except on diplomatic excursions. The evanescence of the game as pure pleasure vanished, and his handicap inexorably rose."

Brawn and company continued to dawdle, happily for me. "I know the area, sir. Not for golf, of course, but rather because of a special breed of sailfish along that coast." He eyed me again. The points in common continued.

"Yes, when I was a boy I used to wonder if they could see us up on the fairways; that 'finny tribe' lurking beneath the green waves." *Windsor Forest.* These literary references continued to astonish me. Brawn was leaving the green, triumphantly waving his ball aloft.

"But all that was long ago," Mark mused, half aloud.

"If I may say so, sir, it seems like yesterday to me," said $12K.

"But then only a sixty-year-old can tell you just how short life is." Three of us nodded gravely, and then we all laughed uproariously. $6K looked confused, which was quite understandable. It wasn't a joke, of course, just an amusing fact—of life, that is. He was simply not ready for it.

So here we were at Firclad. I could attest to its powers to elicit conversation. What a wonderfully strange place to soak up some Far Eastern history. Golf's fairways yield endless secrets.

"It's an interesting point to review. My father never returned home. Although maybe as the senior naval officer in all South China and the Indian Ocean, he was in the last direful days directed to assume strategic command of all Japanese land forces."

"What did General Tojo think of that?"

"He was outraged, naturally, but it was an imperial directive and Tojo was losing his power then. He lost the premiership soon after. It's hard to imagine today, but with the surrender, many survivors of our Burmese army were then taken under control by French and British colonial administrators and used for their purposes."

"What was the idea there?" I queried, glancing back into the *mahonia aquafolia* where I detected some movement among the spiny leaves.

"You know the European colonial powers had nothing much available to them in the Far East after the war except prestige. That is, they were the winners in the southeast, but they had little manpower there. Instead of sending our troops home, they used a large part of them to fight off a new threat: the guerrilla troops of the French-trained Ho Chi Minh. On the other hand, your President Roosevelt had long believed the people of French Indo-China should be free."

This was certainly news to me, and I'm sure to most other persons. But Mark was now engrossed in his next shot, a perfect stroke through the soft air to a favorable site just beyond the pin. His countenance was clearing, too.

"When my father's ashes were finally returned home, as was customary, there was also a letter and a package directed to me. As well, my next older surviving brother inherited the title and what few financial resources were available to us then. But because of stressful war service, his strength was also failing. Would you believe I then received my father's Scottish putter and a wonderful page of Japanese calligraphy, which I think might have surprised and pleased Walter Hagen, among others. They both hang in my private office in Tokyo today, to the astonishment of some of my corporate friends.

Father's legacy, in the best Japanese calligraphic script: 'Always take some time to smell the flowers.' Thus said your great champion, Walter Hagen. A universal philosophy. . . . And do you know what the second might be?" He critically examined my stance.

"Well, I would suppose it had to do with topography."

"You're right," the champion said, 'This is my lie, and I have to do the best I can with it' . . . but there was a more remarkable statement which I don't have in my office. I carry it with me . . . perhaps you will recognize it as something Maudie might have sent on to my father in our family mail during those last chaotic days. Pater hand-rewrote it with his own pen, although we could see he was suffering physical decline. Please try me out on this, Tom." I marveled at their easy first-name basis, which is frankly not my way. "You might know the lines."

"I will, Mark," said I, with not a little wonderment. The note read:

These men, and those who opposed them
And those whom they opposed
Accept the constitution of silence
And are folded in a single party.

How curious! I chipped on to the green a reasonable distance from the cup, still immersed in the density of the statement I had just heard. Then I countered, with some honest pride.

"Yes, I know it . . . very well. An Anglo-American sentiment of sorts. Was it signed . . . that is, identified?"

"No, there was nothing to indicate Marvell, Defoe, Dryden, or . . . anyone. Neither Browne, Vaughan, or any of the great metaphysicals."

"I think Maudie could have told your father it was T.S. Eliot, maybe with a slight Japanese twist to allow for the brush strokes."

He smiled obliquely as he holed out his putt. "Another birdie. How extraordinary! That and the resolution of a great mystery."

The rest of us had pars, which was perhaps just right. At least I decided so later on. But now it was the end of our play together. Pleased as I was, I had made other plans, special and long-standing.

"I thoroughly enjoyed our play, gentlemen, and this meeting. Again, it's one of the unexpected pleasures of golf." There were handshakes all around.

Mark said, "There is every possibility that we will meet again. If you can believe it, we are actually here because of a computer error in my Tokyo office. The printout said eighteen holes, of which I truly see only nine; and my office interpreted two hundred to mean the daily green fees, where I see now it means the *annual* dues!" His was a look between quizzical and incredulous.

"I don't know whether I should comment upon our genuine disbelief or our genuine pleasure." He gazed southerly, down toward the noble river. "Perhaps next time we can, with Izaak Walton, enjoy a discourse on rivers."

"Well, it also means that we do have two hundred members, more or less," said I, getting back on the point. "But we hope for more." Did I look hopeful? Mark turned to walk up to our clubhouse.

"There are simple problems to consider, such as micturation, and then we'll quickly push on to the top five. There's just time."

As they disappeared into the pro shop, Mac clambered up the path behind me.

"Well, what do you think?" He was just a little excited.

"No. They are not here to evaluate your golf course, Mac. He's not going to make an offer you couldn't refuse. But I would think any other idea might be entertained. Scoot on up there!" Which he did with his usual speed. A weekend to remember.

A POSTLUDE

L
ater that afternoon, as I finished my purchases at the hardware store down beside the old river landing, I noted a helicopter cruising downstream. The pilot took a heading up along the hillside toward the golf course and its parking lot. How Juanita would like that! I could easily imagine who his passengers might be—very soon speeding off upriver to a waiting jet.

When I reached home with my more "irresistible" new lures and some even heavier sturgeon line, L.P. had the picnic supper and rods ready down at the pier. The sky was clearing, but there was no sign of an evening breeze as yet.

"I'm dying to get going, but Mac just called for you. He's pretty eager, so I said you'd get right back to him."

I munched on some smoked salmon while the call went through. Juanita answered. "Oh, Tom, just a minute. Mac just went out the door. I'll wave at him."

I could hear her "yoo-hoo!" and imagined her apron fluttering in the breeze.

"Thanks for calling back, Tom."

Tom! How had they found that out?

"You're right, I wanted to tell you that your friends this morning weren't here to buy my course." He sounded relieved, actually. "However, I have just signed up three new members."

"Oh, good," I exclaimed. And I was genuinely pleased. "You will like them."

"Actually, only one of your foursome became a member. The player from the great old tournament course near Kyoto. But he joined as a life member." There was a pause. "Our first, actually. He also asked me to confirm the fact that he was requesting three life memberships. One for himself, and two for you and the missus."

I was speechless. I noodled furiously, wondering what to say, what to think. This was more than a departure. But ye gods! Since when were there life memberships at Firclad? Of course, Mac was also the membership chairman. . . .

"And you can imagine how I feel, Vip—I mean, Tom. I wrote up the certificates right then, banking on your approval. This is $15,000 I didn't have yesterday. . . ." He was sensing my silence and some odd vibes. He expanded, "With this, I can buy a new set of mowers . . . and still put in the putting green I saw you looking for yesterday." What could I say? He and I both know the well-established principle that silence means consent. And $5,000 life memberships—definitely a new category . . . and a new financial position for Juanita and Mac.

"And your man Mark said he had never talked so much or played so well. Two consecutive birdies he reported . . . the older chap was from the Department of Commerce. He said, 'Let me prove it to you,' and he bought all my golf balls, new and used. He called it a 'transaction.'"

"How about the other one?"

"He seemed a bit depressed, somehow, and not at all eager to return to the Department of State. But in the space of our five-minute conversation he said one thing several times."

"Oh, really? Give me some idea."

"He said, 'Up until today, this game hasn't meant all that much to me! I could take it or leave it. It wouldn't have bothered me if I never played again. Ever.'"

"He did?"

"And the other fellow, Mark, said 'Your friend Vip gave me a new insight.' He said you told him to play each shot. Forget about the holes and the score. Did you tell him that?"

"Well, yes. I think I did."

"Well, you're right, of course. That's the secret. One of the big ones, anyway."

"Good! I'm glad, because that's my scheme from now on."

"And he also said that he and Jeremiah would be back to Firclad as soon as possible 'once the vision thing is finally cleared up.' He said you would know what they meant by that."

I thought maybe Mac hadn't talked this long on the telephone for a while. I was getting a bit restive as well, despite all his fascinating news, but we made tentative plans for a game "sometime soon." No point in rushing a good thing, after all.

But then I suddenly remembered my last odd point.

"Say, Mac, I much enjoyed seeing all the players in the tournament play. Congratulations!"

"Actually, we had a narrow win. They have one player who could almost go on the tour."

A POSTLUDE

"Brawn" instantly came to mind. He seemed to have all the points.

"Was he playing just ahead of me part of the time? The young guy with the perfect swing?"

"Yeah, I think he was. But he's not that young anymore. He must be pushing fifty, but he keeps in wonderful shape all year."

"That's the one. Tall and very well turned out?"

"Right. 'Smoky' is meticulous about clothes. He always wears red or black on the course and dark blue suits at the office. Ever since I've known him."

"That's interesting. Where did he come from?"

"He didn't. He was practically born on the golf course up there."

"No kidding! Well, I'd like to meet him sometime. He seemed familiar."

"Yes . . . I can imagine. Well, he's in the telephone book: John Smith, but 'Smoky' might as well be his real name. Why don't you think about that a little bit when you're chopping wood. Remember, the articulated swing." But I was unresponsive. There seemed to be nothing very substantial to work with there, although it seemed that Mac was somehow working with a broad hint. He pursued the matter a bit. "Think back to something tried and true . . . the old interlocking grip." Suddenly it hit me. Talk about full circle! And remembering Beldon, I was neither shocked nor surprised.

But now I could see L.P. through the window, reading a book and patiently idling the little engine beside our dock.

When I finally got the sturgeon rods together and reached the float, L.P. was engrossed in her field glasses. I reported our new memberships. She said, "I should gather I get lifetime lessons at this rate, and right-hand-ed ones, too!"

I detached us from our float, and *Merlin* eased her way down into the mainstream current. L.P. and I enjoy just floating, silent, identifying once again with the great river of time. L.P. had earlier identified this mood for us. I had gone for John Dryden and his Thames ferryman, but L.P. said no; let's go with Samuel Clemens and the wondrous impression of Huckleberry Finn floating downriver at dawn on the Father of All the Waters. "Not a sound anywhere . . . it was so still and sounds came so far . . . and you see the mist curl up off the water, and the east reddens up . . . and next you've got the full day, and everything smiling in the sun, and the song birds just going it." Yes, that's what we had; and we knew it as we floated along the densely covered bank. I thought hard about Mark Twain, and of Melville and the people of his "watery world."

L.P. continued to inventory the glorious wetland vegetation overwhelming the river banks and hills with leaf and blossom. The names were an incantation to Mother Nature: Redberry elder, thimbleberry and goatsbeard, stink currant, Big Root, and false bugbane. "Wild carrot," I exclaimed.

"Or Queen Anne's lace," offered L.P. "And yellow arum!" she added.

"Skunk cabbage," said I.

"Or *Lysichitum americanum*," overcorrected L.P. I could see salmonberries and banks of salal. High on a rocky spur we both spotted the bright blue of Menzies larkspur and some patches of wild roses. A glittering pheasant feasted on an early youngberry and then called for hens.

Towering cedars and firs sat among the vine maple; long, foot-like roots resting deep in the tidewater. And some of the maple leaves were already turning flame red. They had only been in leaf a few days. Too transitory, by far.

L.P. had sculled us into the strong ebb tide and eyed the electric starter, but I felt no need for the motor just yet. The current was running a strong five knots. But L.P. was murmuring something under her breath. I finally got the fact of a past-due lunch; long-delayed, thanks to my socializing.

"This will probably be your meal of the day," pronounced the feigning golf widow. "Lunch has ordinarily been served between 12:00 noon and 2:00, but I know this was a special day."

No wonder I was so hungry. It was well after 5:00.

"You're so right, and I am truly sorry. Perhaps we should call this a cream tea." Our mood changed in the eddying current.

"Funny thing. I've been thinking about the sturgeon that escaped you yesterday morning. Anyway, I want you to get one about seventy inches long—or more, if possible."

L.P. looked enigmatic. "Another fish, if you don't mind. I have one or two ideas about it, if you would like to row down to your famous ninety-eight-foot hole." She chuckled.

While we floated toward that secret spot beneath the fern-clad cliffs, I devoured lunch. First, to whet my hunting urge, L.P. handed me some smoked sturgeon. There were also some very specially prepared, very thin, breast of chicken sandwiches, with arugula and watercress from our sequestered bed, and just for me, a coating of salted butter. My chef had also concocted a container of Greek salad, redolent of fresh basil from her garden, and a perfectly chilled bottle of Sancerre. Aside from some fresh, cold lemonade, there was also a little box of strawberries with powdered sugar—a little—and some lemon tarts, easily washed down by yours truly. Last, but maybe even best, some huge, dark red Bing cherries had been conjured from some immoderately early orchard. Food for a monarch.

On the strength of these Epicurean treatments, I launched into my bear story. My timing was obviously off. L.P.'s features turned ashen, emphasized against the teal green water and the *chatoyence* of the eastern sky.

"Holy Moses!" croaked my pal. My casual approach had failed miserably, so I switched about and began to recount the further incident at Firclad. I described the unlikely golfing trio as I rigged our lines and dropped the nine-ounce weights and our anchor line sixteen fathoms down. It was a good thing I shifted topics, because L.P. continued to gasp. It's always a good thing to have a follow-up story. But then I suddenly began to shake. Could it have been delayed shock as I recalled dirty gray claws, inches long, and slobbering yellow teeth? But then L.P. laughed hugely, deep down. Was it the trailing skunk cabbage?"

You know, with all your offhand ways and odd sense of *politesse*, within a two-day period, you flagrantly violated two of the ancient and sacred golf rules laid down by St. Andrews Club."

"Oh?" said I, astonished.

"I refer to rules ten and eleven. Two big ones."

After an intense moment I said, "Oh yes, rule ten. That must refer to Lucky Pierre's hoof print . . . is that it?"

"Well, possibly. You surely recall how it goes. 'If a ball is stopped by any Person, Horse, Dog, or anything else, the Ball must be played where it lies.'"

"Well, I think that's fine for the honorable company of St. Andrews, but not at Firclad, with the accentuated hoof prints of a behemoth like Lucky Pierre's. . . . What's the other one?" No point in budging on point one.

"You remember that rule eleven states, 'If you draw your Club in order to strike and proceed so far in the stroke as to be bringing down your Club—if then your Club shall break in any way it is to be account-ed a stroke.' So . . . my question to you, dear Thomas, is: did you enter a stroke in your card for that very special bear stroke?" She guffawed, and I joined.

I was saved from falling out of the boat laughing by a tremendous tug on the other side—jerking, emphatic, heavy, and purposeful. Forty tired and exciting minutes later I drew a big log of a fish up beside *Merlin*, float-ing toward us in ghastly prehistoric splendor. One big sturgeon. Hundreds of rough, plated scales.

"It's a seventy-one-inch sturgeon," hooted L.P. "Pull it up here over the gunnel or whatever this is!" she ordered.

Jehoshophat! Easier said than done. Fortunately, I now had heavy can-vas gloves in my sturgeon gear. As I grunted and flopped it half over the side in a torpid slant on the bottom slats, L.P. quick as a flash opened its belly. Ye gods! She quickly ran her sharp skinning knife along and popped out a long, waxy sac looking like oil skins for golf caps. It was bulging with roe, and the big, rough-coated beast appeared inert and unfeeling. Within ten seconds, L.P. had drawn her needle case from her bag and begun deftly sewing two or three layers of incision in the leviathan's stomach with a sail maker's needle. It was mind blasting. What would a game warden think of all this? Rather unexpected.

"Quickly. Turn him back into the water . . . I mean her."

She swam off sedately . . . or maybe moodily.

"What on earth!" I exclaimed. "Now what! Did anyone see us? We could be arrested!"

"Certainly not! This is simply a Swedish trick which I heard about in Malmö. Evidently it's saving the Russian caviar industry in the Caspian. The fish simply descends to the nether regions to review the experience and, if temperate, lives through another cycle. I call it pooching, not poaching."

I noted that L.P. had clipped the suture like a surgeon and given the patient an encouraging pat as it disappeared into the green. Certainly I was ready to join her team.

"So now, *tovarisch*, we can conduct our first experience in making world-class caviar. Let's head for home."

Yes, I was speechless, but also relieved. I was in no shape to fillet a 120-pound fish . . . or maybe 150.

And as L.P. so charitably pointed out, she had left half the eggs. I decided to check all late summer catches of sturgeon for scar tissue, and in the meantime I thought about caviar. Boy, oh boy.

L.P. wrapped her prize in a large compress and laid it on the ice. "About five hundred dollars in Manhattan," said she, reading my mind.

"More like fifteen hundred," I volunteered.

Quiet had begun to fall around us. I was guiding on a point of land ahead and rising up above us from the stream. It was a favorite, for we had learned that the redoubtable Captain Vancouver, R.N., had sent a boat into the Columbia River In 1792, a banner year, and from our very own point of land they had named many streams, islands, hills, and mountains spreading out miles before their wondering eyes.

Meandering vines of honeysuckle and roses gone wild perfumed the evening breeze.

"A century ago, exasperated salmon gillnetters used to litter the sandbars and banks with sturgeon that fouled their nets." I further stated, "Of course they were simply thought of as nuisance fish. There were no Russians or Persians about then. And everyone knew that salmon runs would last forever."

A POSTLUDE

As we neared our float in the dusk, I could see someone pacing back and forth in the waning light. An already familiar figure. "Ahoy there, Mac! How did you find us down here in our bivouac?"

"Well, I just took a chance, Vip. I hope you two don't mind. I had to see you because I've just come on the darnedest thing ever, something to be shared with you two right now." He could scarcely suppress his excitement.

"Well, good! Let's sit up here on the deck with a beaker of single malt."

"Say, that's great. I knew you would respond. And just a little spring water in my dram, if you please."

"Let's make it three," said L.P., heading for the refrigerator and some heavy glasses. Our water spews from the side of a huge forest-clad hill, hard and hearty. Within minutes we were hunkered down, looking west toward trailing streaks of vermilion sunset. Mac drank deep and launched into the story he was obviously bursting to tell.

"Listen, guys, this is one for Ripley. You simply won't believe it. Like lots of Scots, my dad expected to wander, so he kept a journal. Something really curious about this afternoon suddenly clicked in my mind, so I went down to our storage to forage a bit in his old trunk."

He savored the scotch, knowing he had instantly captured our historically heightened attention in a way that easily outstripped the magical evening. Even Addison at his best.

"You know, my father was a habitual golfer. Some persons call it the Scottish disease, but they're wrong. It's just a very strong habit. Be that as it may, his other love was steam engineering. Marine boilers, to be more precise, or specific. He was a civilian, but he had done much overseeing work for old Jackie Fisher when he was in the mood, the brilliant and mad admiral who built *Dreadnought*."

L.P. and I knew something about the famous battleship and could nod familiarly. He plowed on.

"In August of 1912, Big Mac, as they called him, was on the train going down through Carlisle to Morecombe Bay to look at some boiler problem or other. He was a bachelor then. He had his golf bag with him when he bounded into a compartment on the little spur train off from Carlisle to Whitehaven in Cumbria. Rather surprisingly for those times, there was an Asian already seated there in empty First Class. He was dressed in plus fours, and a very new set of golf clubs was drawn up next to him almost like mascots. Well, like your own Siberian train passengers, they very soon got to talking golf. I remember now my dad telling me years ago that the next thing he knew they had stepped down from the train for the shore of Whitehaven and began to play a links course.

"His new companion had come down from Troon, where he had played in some pretty fancy company. But now here's the thing. He told Dad that his name was Mark, just like your gentleman from Japan this afternoon! So I just had to check it out. And Vip, you should see the entries. They played every golf course from Maryport to Whitehaven, and in the August wind, too. And there were other notes. . . . Mark had started to play somewhere in Scapa, then at Invergordon, Bridge of Orchy and Dunbarton, and then on to Royal Dornoch and at Irvine, Ayr, and Prestwick, as well as Lockerbie and Dumfries, just above Carlisle."

The names rolled from his lips. Great old names carried around the world. After all, our John Paul Jones first sailed out of Whitehaven. Talk about a tough school for sailors. But Mac was in full fettle, and golf was his theme.

"What a meeting, especially since my pa said he soon found out they were both in naval construction and engineering. So they went on to play at Corcickle and the dear little seaside links at St. Bees; not to mention Netherstown, Braystones, Sellafield, Seascape, Drigg, Ravenglass, and several others."

"That's a lot of diary entries!" I exclaimed. But Mac was mixing a second glass of malt.

"As far as I can determine, they must have stopped briefly at the naval yard in Morecombe Bay as a matter of form. They both had some duty obligations there. The next day they played on through, ending mid-week at Preston and Chester. Twenty-eight courses in all, and some days they played three different courses. But then my dad returned to Morecombe, and Mark continued on from Chester to London."

"It all sounds wonderfully impulsive," said L.P., just a bit wistfully.

"Impulsive, you say. That's not the half of it, Missus. My old man went back to Seascape, where they had played four rounds. On the last hole that late afternoon, he had spotted his future bride, a mysteriously beautiful young woman seated in a luxuriant dark green garden of a summerhouse between the Irish Sea and the rolling fairways. My mother had long, radiant, red hair, and I guess she was taking her ease drying it in the sun and wind while she pored over her morning golf score. Suddenly he appeared over the hedge. Lochinvar of the Links. Can you imagine!"

"It was meant to be," sighed L.P.

"Sorcery," I thought.

"You've heard of the French thunderclap, I'm sure," queried Mac. We nodded with enthusiasm. Love at first sight.

"I mean he fell in love at 407 yards! Burnished Danegeld, he called it. Just imagine!"

L.P. could easily imagine. She tossed her grand mane a bit; definitely gold. Sometimes the world drenches itself in romance. Complete immersion.

"But here's the long arm of coincidence stretched longer . . . why I'm here talking and drinking so much of your fine liquor. You see right here? Here's my dad's journal with his friend's signature and address in the flyleaf, and here is our register from Firclad." Mac busily flipped through the pages of his own book.

"So read us what you've found," I suggested.

"I can't. That's just it. Both entries are in Japanese script, but the journal has a roman IV and the registry has a roman V, plus the two bohunks from Washington."

"Not to worry," I said. "L.P. will no doubt make some sense of it. She likes these puzzles."

He nodded appreciatively, having earlier realized her endless resources and possibilities.

"So what's the secret, L.P.?"

"Actually, there's no name here, Vip—I mean Tom. There's a kind of code message in his signature, Mac, and the journal entry is very obviously his father's. But his cryptic entry translates simply: 'Jolly good show! Thank you! *I shall return.* And soon. Mark V.'"

We were bound to laugh. A famous phrase, that.

"He goes on, however, in straight script. 'I foresee that we shall someday play the classic eighteenth hole at Kasunigaseke . . . later on in our lives.' That's it."

"Funny," said Mac, "I know that course. I'm surprised he didn't choose the fourteenth, a real bearcat. It's just seven yards short of 600. And speaking of short, he might have mentioned the grounds staff the greenskeeper has there. Over two hundred."

I had been silent, ruminating. "Mac, I think he now prefers zest to grooming. So your Firclad triumphs. What a very curious turn of affairs.

We sprawled about on the big deck, exclaiming and reviewing the several pleasures of the last two days. The ardent sun had plunged well west of Astoria, dropping fast toward Japan to rise from an ocean once again. The broad waters of our noble river provided matchless and reassuring views prodigally enhanced by the last glides and plunges of eagles, osprey, kingfishers, and stealthy herons. So altogether right it was that we helped ourselves to another short peg of the best with some slices of sablefish, sturgeon, and salmon cheeks.

Once more we took our ease to review the unbelievable two days that we had just experienced and assess what seemed to be an increasing number of incredible lies; golf was beyond conception, beyond most imaginations. My Life Partner pronounced that the gods very obviously continued to walk with us, which meant we should tread even more softly in the days ahead. Harmony with them transcended all earthly affairs. Mac agreed and smiled in anticipation, left-handed, of course. He stretched archly and then opined:

> By the yard, life is hard,
> but inch by inch, it's a cinch.

L.P. clapped hard for this basic rubric, a gem. But I returned the volley through the dusk:

> Know that golf's a heartless joke,
> unless you love it stroke by stroke.

As we regaled ourselves with wit and sallies (or so it seemed at the time), a light mist eddied upstream on spring breezes from the shoreline. We were gradually enveloped in a refreshingly cool mist. Mac suddenly told us about how his dad had been killed. "It was in the war," he said, "but it was actually and incredibly on the ninth hole at Ravenglass. A prowling 109E Messerschmidt swept out of the clouds to shoot up yet another rail station and the waiting engines and cars. In a burst of ill humor, the obviously non-golfing pilot had also shot up the ninth green and everyone on it. Happily, Dad had just established a course record that still stands, I'm told; but it was a lousy tradeoff for a sixty-year-old man. He had worked every day since August 1939, with a few rounds sneaked in at dusk."

We fell silent again, pondering the vagaries of life and curiously sudden mists. "What's the famous Oregon mist doing over here?" I quipped. "What about the boundary line?" As we withdrew toward light and warmth, L.P. dependably added, "I bet there's a name for this mist in Scotland."

"Oh yes," said Mac. "They call it a har. My old granddad used to say he'd had his fill of the har up to hyar."

Frankly, I prefer another kind of mist; and so we had some of those, too. It seemed just right with a McClelland base.

But then the urgent moon soared over the har from the east, again turning the roadstead into shivering platelets of gold and tourmaline. I was reminded of my second-best ever, nine-hole score, before "the second war." My next younger brother, John, had the preceding day once again won the boys' state-wide championship. A week earlier my next older brother had won the junior championship in the state to our south, with a playoff in the late autumn sun. They were both fiercely fought matches, and my brothers were elated, if not jubilant. I had never won a big championship nor any medals or trophies, and they were understandably a bit full of themselves. Their schedules were all penciled in for the next month or so, and I was leaving to pursue other interests. I challenged them then and there to a family game with our dad. Right then and there. It was past nine o'clock, and poor old Dad had to rise from bed to placate his energized falcon children.

"But how could you play?" exclaimed L.P. "The summer light would have faded by then."

"Actually, it was late fall. Now, if you can believe this, the first odd spray of snow crystals had rimed all the fairways and greens. Like angels' wings, all feathery light and white for miles. The course was at about eighteen hundred feet."

"I can't believe this," said Mac.

"Oh I can," purred L.P. "Plunge on."

"Well, it's a simple but wonderful story of youth. Just as we reached the darkened first tee in our heavy sweaters and knickers, an absolutely vast and splendrous hunter's moon floated up from the black and silent hills. They were still covered with magnificent old-growth trees then, which gave everybody and every shadow a sharper definition . . . even our lives, maybe."

"So you played nine holes by moonlight? Boy, that's a new one. But how did you see your ball, Vip?" Mac was with it.

"Well, we were young, first off, and full of bliss and confidence, and a vision more than 20/20. My dad and I waxed them six on three; and I also won the medal play at one under. Believe it, a very critical game in my life; but still no trophy. And as I said, I won the medal play by three strokes. I still have two or three red balls from that game lurking about, but they both have cases of trophies and sweet memories, not to mention Richard and Gerald."

"It's almost unbelievable," burred Mac.

"Oh, I believe it," L.P. said without pause. No surprise there. "I could have told them that you play your best in the moonlight in a light snow."

A fetching thought, that, as usual. "Very flattering," I stated factually.

We were all caught again in a timeless moment of blissful content. Happily, we knew it. That's always the best part of those moments. We made some plans for the days ahead, including L.P.'s lessons. Three a week. Then Mac left us, as usual in a half-lope.

Happily I fell into a soundless sleep that night, but very early next morning I experienced an intense dream. We had all begun walking down from Edinburgh to Berwick to London. Mac, L.P., and I were in company with the nice young crown prince, Charles; Charles Stuart, that is. It seemed quite natural to be carrying our golf clubs, playing an uninterrupted game as we sauntered south over the hills and dales and down into the lowlands. In our foursome, I drove across the Tweed at Berwick as we headed toward Blackheath and the court of Charles' father, James the First, formerly the sixth Edward in the Scottish line of kings. It was all quite wonderful: sublime mornings, fine picnic lunches, long and spacious afternoons, plus some memorable shots. We made our own rules, and we played well and steadily, although Charles had moments of caprice. It was springtime in 1603, in a great new reign. It was grand to be alive and well. No one gave thought to the years ahead.

I have this kind of dream beside our noble river. To say the least, it keeps me in a state of wonderment about past lives. To have lived before seemed unlikely . . . and yet . . .

As we moved down past Berwick toward Newcastle, the Prince was playing especially well. At Hadrian's ancient Roman Wall, a large band of men had gathered. They were armed with golf clubs of every description.

There were many huzzahs and sounds of exultation as they clamored around our royal party. Then as one they fell in behind us, in the English manner, and began to play golf with us down toward Lincoln and Manchester. Here and there we stopped to look at paintings, the young prince's second interest. . . .

I woke up to a pleasant, mist-filled morning. I simply couldn't believe how stiff I was. Every bone, every muscle, and everything else. Like a mummy. No one ever, to my knowledge, warns new gray panthers about this sorry plight. Looking down the long, almost limitless marine green view toward the Pacific surf, I ruminated through the mist runnels on the attractions of senior status. Oh, they are there all right, although some parts on occasions seemed much overvalued.

On the other hand I noted, just as an immense osprey plummeted into the frothy tide below our windows, there was more than enough to savor. After all, just how long had it been since I had played eighteen holes on foot; that is, a true round, and on a hillside yet? And who could have been more theatrical or, more specifically, more erratic? The female osprey missed her fish by one talon, which caused me to think about some of my own misses. I heard her vexed cry. A reminder to keep my mouth shut even as the years pile up.

Now there *was* a very defined area where I could surely improve, no doubt about it. Fanning the ball was unnerving. There was not only the hideous embarrassment to consider, there was something equally palpable: the strokes. Hamlet was right. Then too, "a miss is as good as a mile" still holds true and always will. As well, the stress factor is a consideration; perhaps distress is the better word, psychologically speaking. Just thinking about missing, to the exclusion of all other things, surely causes mental damage, if not hardship.

INCREDIBLE LIES

So I decided that the facts of life as I viewed them demanded that I resolve—nay, that I conquer—this particular insidious problem. "Today's game must be played today," was my motto—and with today's strokes. And from now on I would include one practice swing, at least on the tees. Not for me the piteous memory of an earlier decade when I had come upon a book entitled *Thirty Years of Looking Up*. That was more about self-flagellation than golf swings.

Buoyed up with these self-healing notions, I once more repaired to the wood yard, where I continued a pre-breakfast review of the astonishing holes of golf played over the last two days, including Mac's game, of course. And Lucky's contributions as well. My Titleist in Lucky Pierre's hoof print was a "forever" in my memory book.

It reminded me as well of a wonderfully gregarious Yale savant, Billy Phelps. He took up golf late, forsaking lawn tennis. At the turn of our century (the twentieth century, that is), he and his faculty cronies played every week of the year, whatever the season and the weather. Phelps reported that hip boots and red balls were employed during the long New Haven winters. Most important to me, William Lyons Phelps played simply to have a good time. Closer to my memory, however, was his report from a western auto trip. In North Dakota, a local scorecard (not a links, obviously) which instructed that "Balls rolling into gopher holes may be dropped without penalty." Phelps was that honestly odd type of New England sophisticate; but I know that Firclad's rules on elk hoof prints would have thrown Billy off the pace, not to mention the herds of deer stalking Mac's fairways.

As I gnawed on these singularities, I quickened the strokes of my singing, double-bitted ax. It helped me to focus some thoughts about my swing in terms of relatively pure physics. Proud as I am of my swing in its natural form, with the decades perhaps some reassessment was needed;

even to the point of seeking professional help, a procedure I had seldom submitted to in my life.

Giving it further thought, I reviewed the simple mechanics of the pendulum. My club length, as far as I could determine, is about sixty-four inches, swinging in an arc. The vibrations of the pendulum are as the square roots of their lengths. For example, the length of a pendulum that will vibrate seconds in New York, at the level of the sea in Manhattan, is 39.1013 inches. This I turned over in my mind as my morning mental exercise: how many vibrations my swing, as a pendulum, would make in a minute, knowing that as the square root of the length of the pendulum is to sixty-four, so is the square root of 39.1013 to the number of vibrations required? To do this, one must take eight (the square root of 64):60::6.25 (the square root of 39.1013), yielding 46.875 vibrations, as nearly as I could figure. However, in that split second of producing the answer, I narrowly missed chopping my foot. It seemed wiser to think about other things. Thoughts about Mark came tumbling out. Now here was a special case.

He had briefly mentioned that his own favorite American military hero, as opposed to his father's stable of favorites, was a lesser-known rear admiral in World War II, C.A.F. Sprague.

Mark told me, "There is no doubt in my mind that Sprague saved your Admiral Halsey's reputation, plus many of his ships off Samar in the Second Battle of Leyte Gulf. He deserves serious reevaluation, as do the brave crews of his light carrier force."

Mark realized that my impressive body of information on this extraordinary—bordering on ominous—engagement did not rival his; and he courteously concluded by saying, "Clifton Sprague was a golfer too, of sorts, but more to the point, he saved my life. When his six light carriers and seven destroyers threw themselves into the face of our four giant battleships, our entire force, including four cruisers and eleven crack destroyers, turned away. By that action, Admiral Kurita in essence said 'the naval war is finished.' He disbelieved in kamikaze tactics, thank the gods, so my naval air unit was consequently disbanded rather than sacrificed to pride. With the collapse of the Sho Plan we were all sent to raise rice for the invasion everyone knew was coming. All the glory went to Sprague's 'Taffy Three.' He saved the American invasion fleet."

While I mulled over these once-obscure facts, Mark withdrew into memory. Toward the end of our meeting, however, I asked him what had taken such deep reflection, thinking that he might reveal something more about his career and present plans. But no.

"I've been thinking about this most interesting golf course, Tom, and its general layout; what I'm wondering is how Firclad would fit into the Japanese landscape."

"Well," I pondered, "I don't think it would, at least not in any reasonable way."

Mark agreed. "I share your view. I've given some thought to the course, based on the first four holes. Feel free to interrupt; but as I see it, the eighteen holes, so called, truly are nine, comprising the probable trapezoid making up the lower holes we are playing, and something approaching an irregular polygon making up the top five. I know that your famous American township is six miles square, containing thirty-six sections; a total of 23,040 acres." I saw no point in interrupting this discourse.

Mark pressed on. "While a section comprises one square mile of land, or six hundred forty acres, a quarter section is half a mile square, totaling one hundred sixty acres. I took the first fairway, which is long and irregular, to be about eighty rods long and at about ten-rod intervals are about eight, ten, eleven, nine, eight, seven, nine, and ten rods in breadth, which comes to around four and one-half acres if we agree that twelve rods ten feet and eight and one-half inches make one acre. A rice field the size of this course, which must be about forty acres all told, might produce enough food for a Japanese town of eight thousand people or so. Do you see?"

"Yes, I get your point. There's more land here, and an easier attitude toward it." There was little else to say on so short a meeting.

"Well, actually, this exercise is pointless, since the whole course runs along hillsides, and rice production demands level fields, banked up and full of water." He laughed hard.

Fortunately, I hadn't interrupted this stream of consciousness disquisition on land use, and there was no need for further commentary; certainly nothing aloud. As with so much, it was academic.

But what an engaging chap! So far I had not had the right opportunity to fill Mac in on all that I had learned, especially some aspects of the phenomenal Cumbrian coincidence. It was in every way a series of meetings defying analysis. Descartes would have thrown up his hands.

So I reconsidered my swing. If I could just slow down the backswing aspect *on every stroke* and reinstate my once formidable putting prowess, I might begin to think of the inscrutable Walter J. Travis as my exemplar. "Black Walter" was a titan, beating the British squarely at their own game in 1924. A significant year, that.

Throughout this career, Travis played in a dour, rigid manner, adhering absolutely to the rules. After putting, as his sometime partner in later years Billy Phelps once noted, he always stood still watching his ball "pursue its inexorable course." In other words, he never followed his ball toward the cup or jumped on the green. Would that some today might emulate and stop jumping up and down on the greens!

How pleasing it would be to have one or two treasured lines from Travis' British-written obituary incorporated into one's own. For *The Times* eulogist remarked, "I have never seen, however, such utter consternation as was produced by Mr. Travis' putting in that final round at Sandwich, nor any putting that had about it such a suggestion of black magic . . . still as a statue, watching the ball with those inscrutable eyes . . . he seemed a wizard to be burned at the stake. As a game player he had essential greatness." The British are not poor losers, but often they are definitely hard losers. Travis was the first "cousin" to triumph over them; and those were words of praise to pant after; but then, too, Travis played at least once every day. Paderewski was so right: "Practice is all."

Such thoughts of long ago put me in mind of the eventual fate of caddies, and what caddying meant to young lads in the early years. Today's reality is not about their future fate but their present demise, especially for youngsters. The only ones we now see are the major domos profitably packing around in the blaze of television, accompanying their star players to an ever increasing number of manicured courses decorating our Earth. So another important opportunity lost with changing times, not only to earn some money and get a leg up, but even more important, to observe men and women close up and under some pressure. How revealing it can be, human nature, close up.

In my own case, some local championships I saw played out in the hard rain and hot sun of distant years are forever embedded as childhood memories. There were very odd things some persons said and did when things went wrong; and the marvelously graceful actions of others when games went even more inexplicably wrong. How instructive it all was, especially to see how volcanic the tiniest person might become, how taciturn the largest.

The utterly splendid Sandy Hurd came to mind from those dusty years before the Great War. He had started out as a caddie at St. Andrews, watching and admiring the old champions and their shots. "It used to give me pleasure when I was old enough to carry their clubs; what an honour I thought it was! Then they used to gather around old Tom Morris' shop at night and talk of the great matches they had played and how they had lost and won championships. I used to stand with my ears and mouth wide open, drinking every word in."

No one could have put it more plainly and with such simple eloquence. Later, in *My Golfing Life*, Alexander Hurd said other things to occupy my thoughts now as I swung my ax, cleanly splitting the alder logs. I reconstructed how his philosophy related to caddies, and players, too. "Golf is a game one must have at heart. One must love it and think it all out as to how to become a champion. One must practice for everlasting, and we can never quite master its wonderful elusive ways."

Old Alex sure had that right. Timeless thoughts for sure. As the chips flew, I thought of a few persons who played some days as much as four or six grim rounds of nine holes, but never revealed a shred of love for the game as we trudged through heat and sleet. It might as well have been the last mile at Ossining. And often their drivers, and especially their putters, had to be retrieved from trees, ponds, nettles, blackberry thickets, and other fairways—sometimes an Olympian toss away. And while they never thought as champions, such bleak folks provided some instruction and much silent laughter.

Interestingly enough, it crossed my mind right then that in those early days, I probably saw more great-hearted women players than men: Muriel, Daisy, Kathleen, Mary, Kathryn, and Hildegarde, not to mention Tracey, Margot, and decidedly yes, Cameron and Meagan too! Such spirit they exhibited; steadfast and unflinching, courteous to a fault, and winners as well. Yes, we could learn about life while on the links, especially if one were gifted with a sense of humor and strong legs.

Our woodpile had grown impressively with all these conjectures, and I began to think this kind of exercise would benefit my heart and soul as well as my joints—the number of which seemed to increase each year. And I could actually feel long-lost strength returning to my wrists. Such good news! Many's the scratch player who has confided to me that the basic secret of golf is the uncocking of one's wrists. So my father had casually opined more than a few years ago, when he conversed on the black arts of perfect timing on the course and off.

The delicious redolence of L.P.'s incomparable Sunday morning breakfast cooking wafted on a runaway shred of mist between the kitchen door and my chopping block. Yes, I was earning that mug of café au lait and those delicate pancakes swimming in berry syrup—all twelve of them. Bacon, too. And butter!

I supposed it was natural that a last thought about Yale golf would come along. After all, it was an anniversary morning, and all seemed right with the world. So guess what? Yes, old Harry Varden in fact played an exhibition match there during his first visit to America. His play that April in 1900 was thought to be miraculous, revelatory. Yale sent up its two finest players, and Harry played their best ball. On the second day he carded a seventy-one, a course record that stood for almost half a century. And yes, he won hands down. A

A POSTLUDE

British bulldog. Bow-wow-wow! Suddenly I remembered my last game at Yale, realizing that I might actually have broken Harry Vardon's record, if I had played safely, striving for a birdie rather than a proud hole in one.

While I shaved I was reminded of other wonderments about the gruff wonder-player from Jersey; but always it reduced to "never stop hitting the ball." We all know that he said that not once but all of the time. I mused in the steam. I knew the Master would understand if I now chose Lord Harry's simple words for my life motto . . . "no matter what happens. . . ." But of course, I needed something else, just a bit more than this, if I were to swear an oath under the double eagle with green-eyed L.P. watching. Every nine is composed of two parts incredible lies and one part strokes of luck—with a dash of bitters. Yes!

I would further swear to strive for holes in one—the ace—wherever physically possible, even after the first one . . . or two or three. Why not? And so would L.P., now that she was starting. She might even beat me . . . and furthermore I would begin to follow the final advice Prince Albert gave to Victoria. Leaving my role as a very private golfer, I would begin to think about playing today's game today rather than dream of future triumphs or brood over past follies—what a grand resolve! I could hardly wait to swear the oath!

It reminded me of a flawless Friday morning in September long ago. Our foursome had set out to play the Vanderbilt's legendary Shinnacock Hills course on Long Island, the gorgeous links that Scots wizard Willie Dunn had so cunningly laid out with the help of 150 Indian braves from a native village nearby. I had just made the Atlantic crossing on the Queen, coming from a game at Royal St. George and a unique golfing experience. I was almost hesitant to tell my old American playing partners about it. But then, one wants to share stories about golf. By the third hole I was in deep trouble. I looked up and drove into the worst bunker of the terrible three which guard the entrance to the long fairway beyond the sea grass. However, I was well into my incredible story of the starting round at St. George . . . and what happened to me and our foursome that day.

Back in those days I imitated the French cannoneers of old who gave every kind of impressive and outrageous names to their artillery pieces. Beyond imagination. But to go on, in the third bunker of the third hole I broke my third iron, "the club of irony." The club head cracked off. I can hear it today. It flew away toward the fourth tee, landing at the feet of a spectator. I was destined to meet L.P.! And naturally, through the years, I would just overhear that irresistible remark: "Tom really lost his head." In the meantime, my new three iron became "the club of destiny." I had experienced a unique stroke of luck.

But now my luck with the double-bitted axe was being pushed and my nose followed the sweet aromas indoors to the kitchen.

Later in the day, during our modest lunch, L.P. added a few drops of absinthe to the oysters Rockefeller. Gazing over the chicken Marengo we spied a gloomy storm ponderously moving upriver. Wicked yellow tongues of lightning leaped from the depths. L.P. was glued to the window as a water spout suddenly formed and faltered. God chatted with Odin, but all was tight and right with our tiny world. L.P. acknowledged the wave of the pilot standing firm on the bridge.

I headed for a deep bath and submerged to my ears thinking about caviar and the spacious evening ahead. Random thoughts about "the club of irony" brought back memories of my treasured five iron. On a whim, I had carried it with me through Yokohama, Nahodka and on the Trans-Siberian rail trip. A weary KGB agent following me around Irkutsk finally sidled up as I examined a broken rain spout flowing along a crack in the sidewalk.

A POSTLUDE

"Is that your golf club?" he asked dubiously.

"Yes, it's mine . . . one of seventeen."

"You own seventeen? You must know Ike then?"

"Oh, yes."

"And Tom Mix . . . and Jeanette McDonald? And Eddy Nelson?"

"Oh, yes. We're all good friends." In for a penny, in for a pound, thought I.

He whispered on through the downpour, "We built a special golf course for Ike in Irkutsk . . ." He frowned . . . "Before u-2."

"Oh, good. Where is it?"

"Well, I don't know . . . it's not played. . . . Some day we'll have more golf sites than America. In ten years, we'll have more autos than you do . . . far more."

He vanished as I wryly remarked, "Good luck." There were no traffic signs or lights in the "Paris of Siberia."

Another memorable dinner with L.P. wound down. True to my rules, only two perfect Manhattans were served up before the entré. Yes, they were small . . . goblet size. In any event I took a plunge and repaired to my small room of "possibles" which our children called Aladdin's. There, among several shelves of left-behinds from those gone ahead, I ferreted out a still-handsome bag. Returning to the main arena, I laid the trophy at L.P.'s feet. With brio, of course.

"Good heavens! What are all these clubs?" she exclaimed.

"Well, I thought you might work your way through them with Mac. When you find some you really like, we can upgrade to this century's clubs."

L.P. observed the stash pensively. A long moment later she climbed the stairs, proclaiming in the ascent, "I shall master all these clubs if it takes from now until Thanksgiving." We both laughed uproariously and fell into bed.

INCREDIBLE LIES

Morning came bright and full of optimism. I saw L.P. off with a flourish to her first lesson with Mac. I busied myself constructing a simple netted driving range for two looking out across the noble river. Nothing like the great three-tiered temple constructions we had gasped over in Japan.

Our driver had casually informed us that most of the men on the driving platforms had no chance to play on a regular course. But we held out great hopes for them anyway.

In the midst of these memories Mark's conversations came up for review. No, he had not quoted Wordsworth's incomparable lines, "The world is too much with us, late and soon . . ." Yet, that is. There *must* be future occasions.

Our wonderful guests would surely return, and the words would flow. And think of it. Three days ago, I had almost left my gift bag of clubs behind for the touted garage sale. And now here I was with a whole new future.

"To retire at the height of one's powers is Heaven's way," an Asian sachem had intoned. And the Master himself extended Lord Harry's statement, saying, "You must keep trying and keep on hitting the ball so that you might enjoy a lucky break." He went on to say that after all, a hundred average players make a hole in one to each expert.

Maybe we are all experts—would Mark and Mac agree? Until we all met again, L.P. and I would keep on striving for strokes of luck . . . and for boundless love of the other great game.

My favorite shots are the practice swing and the conceded putt.
The rest can never be mastered.

LORD ROBERSTON

ABOUT THE AUTHOR

Recognized most prominently as the long-time executive director of the Oregon Historical Society located in Portland, Thomas Vaughan has written many works based on the history of the Northwest and exploration of the Pacific Rim. He has been honored by Queen Elizabeth II and by the Russian Academy of Sciences for his work on international museum and North Pacific studies. He has served on executive committees of the NEH and NEA, as well as three federal and many regional and state commissions. He prizes the vote by the Oregon State Legislature in 1989 unanimously electing him to life honors as Oregon Historian Laureate.

After serving with the Marines of World War II, Vaughan fostered a lifelong interest in military history, particularly maritime history. He has traveled widely with his family, generally with golf bag in tow, and is able to cast a benevolent eye on the foibles of mankind, particularly in reference to odd locations for golf links in strange and unlikely places. He currently spends his time writing and producing books and films.